THE OVERSEAS CHINESE IN ASEAN:
Business Strategies and Management Practices

Victor Simpao Limlingan

Cover Design by Gij Ramos

The Overseas Chinese in ASEAN: Business Strategies and Management Practices

Victor Simpao Limlingan

The objective of this book is to formulate a conceptual framework for explaining how the Overseas Chinese in the ASEAN countries have achieved remarkable economic performance.

The first part of the book deals with validating and accounting for their economic performance. The remarkable economic performance is fact and cannot be explained away by any statistical or structural hypothesis. Moreover, historical analysis indicates that the remarkable performance cannot be explained by the Trader -hypothesis.

The second part deals with stating an alternative hypothesis to the disproven Trader hypothesis. The alternative hypothesis must explain how Chinese businessmen evolved from the migration of coolie laborers. The book explains the remarkable economic performance on the basis of the business policy framework. The economic performance is attributed to the discovery of a superior strategy effectively implemented by a structure flowing from the strategy and consistent with Chinese culture.

The third part deals with a detailed description of the strategy and the structure. The strategy is actually a series of strategies: 1) a first level low-margin/high-volume strategy aimed at achieving a significant market share; 2) a second level strategy based on economies of scope, 3) a third level opportunistic strategy of business deals, and 4) a fourth level strategy dictated by the economic development plans of specific ASEAN countries. The effective structure devised by the Overseas Chinese in ASEAN is built on their twin areas of strength - entrepreneurship and the Chinese culture: 1) the use of social control systems to offset the lack of Western-type control systems, 2) the adoption of an entrepreneurial organization, and 3) the focus on the function of entrepreneurship by family members.

To
Marita
my wife and my beloved

Acknowledgements

This book was written in the afternoon of my life. While hopefully not the culmination of my life's work, this does represent a milestone at which I can privately reflect and publicly acknowledge the people and institutions that have shaped and nurtured my life and this book.

I begin by thanking my parents, Gerardo S. Limlingan, Sr. and Emilia S. Simpao who have served as models for emulation and who have labored to provide me with the best possible education.

I thank my brother, Gerry who upon the untimely death of our father, sacrificed his chances for a higher education by financially supporting his younger, less talented brother. I thank my sister, Josie who brightened my stay in the United States while working and raising a family in Canada.

The writing of a book requires a nurturing institution. I have been fortunate in having three: the Asian Institute of Management, the SGV Group and the Harvard Business School.

I first became interested in the Overseas Chinese in ASEAN when I was a faculty member at the Asian Institute of Management. This interest was encouraged by the Dean of Faculty, Meliton V. Salazar. He approved funding for my research despite the non-case nature of the research and he exiled me with a light teaching load to Indonesia and Malaysia so I could concentrate on writing the initial papers on the Overseas Chinese in ASEAN.

My research interest was further encouraged by the President of the institute, Gabino A. Mendoza. He convinced me that only by writing a doctoral dissertation could I do justice to the subject. He was not only free with his advice, he followed such advice with specific actions. He recommended me to the Harvard DBA program and scrounged around for enough funds from the tight budget of AIM to make my doctoral plan a reality.

I was assured of the support of SGV even before I left for the Harvard Business School. Mr. Roy S. Navarro, the managing partner of the SGV Group promised the support of the SGV Group in all the ASEAN countries for my research effort. In 1984 and in 1985, SGV came through with this support. For this I am grateful, especially to Budiman Elkana of SGV Indonesia, Mar Samaniego of SGV Thailand and Rene Fuentes of SGV Malaysia.

The doctoral program of the Harvard Business School provided me with the academic discipline and atmosphere to write this book. The Division of Research was most understanding in funding my research trips and easing the financial pressures. The DBA staff, Rita

Cherington, Madelyn Kissock, Debbie Mauger and Beverly Davies were most supportive. I will always remember them for teaching me how to operate the copying machine.

My research trips have been most fruitful because of the support of the various people and institutions. I especially wish to thank Djimitra Gandaprawira and his institute, Lembaga Pengembangan Perbankan Indonesia (LPPI) who provided not only the facilities of the institute but also arranged my interviews with Indonesian experts.

My research trips have also benefitted from the help of my former AIM students in the ASEAN region. I wish to express my deep appreciation for the help extended by the MM graduates of Malaysia; John Noel Subramanian, Razali Jaafar, Ismail, Ian Chia, Charlie Cheah, Paul Ng, Anthony Dibble and P. L. Wong.

I was not lacking in support from my AIM colleagues. I thank Frankie and Thelma Roman, Bert Ladores, Bing Azanza, Jim Donelan, Bobby Lim, Vic Lim, Fil Alfonso, Vickie and Klaus Hoffarth, Leni Panganiban, Jess Gallegos, Joe Faustino, Gloria Chan and Nina Cruz-Sy.

Of the many Chinese businessmen who have given generously of their time and knowledge in talking to this researcher, I wish to especially thank Dr. Tan Poh Lin. A practitioner and scholar of Chinese management practices, Poh Lin was both a friend and collaborator in this research effort.

My research efforts generated the necessary data. In converting the data into knowledge, Peter Timmer, my thesis chairman was both a supportive adviser and rigorous critic. I shall never forget the Socratic discussion I had with Jim Austin as we rode the bus from Mont Ste. Marie to Hull. I thank Professor Alfred Chandler. I will always treasure the experience of studying at the feet of the master.

While this book was being written, life went on. My stay in Cambridge was magical. Marita managed our household efficiently in addition to holding a job to support a student-husband and running sorts of errands for the family firm. In this she was greatly helped by Adring Alagos.

My three-year stay at Cambridge was not without cost. I missed the company of my friends in the Philippines. Fortunately, Anthony Aguirre, Bobby Guevara, Gus Lazo, Tol Requesto, Romy Jorge and Mario Labadan appreciated what I had to do. For this, I thank them.

My children; Victor, Regina, Cristina and Luis may be too young to appreciate what I have done. Nevertheless, in the hope that they will one day read this, I thank them for keeping quiet while Papa was working and asking about the progress of the work when Papa was loafing.

This book, like the love poems of my youth, drew its inspiration from Marita, my wife and my beloved. Her love and caring have brought me nothing but happiness. I dedicate this book as I have my life to her.

Cambridge, Massachusetts
May 15, 1986

Table of Contents

List of Tables

List of Figures

FOREWORD

Dr. Victor S. Limlingan admits to being the distant descendant of a *hua-ch'iao*, the term commonly used for Chinese living abroad, and about whom he has undertaken this treatise. He has persuaded me that it is only proper that another such descendant inscribe the foreword.

This book was originally written as a thesis for the Harvard Business School, submitted by the author in partial fulfillment of the requirements for the degree of Doctor of Business Administration, which he received in 1986.

It therefore begins with an exploratory journey through business literature, particularly the history of Business Policy and its evolution into the more current nomenclature, Business Strategy. For faculties of business schools, corporate planners and chief executive officers this first part is an interesting excursion through the contributions of the more famous business writers on this subject.

Even this scholarly introduction, however, already contains insights into the business strategies and management practices of the Chinese who found themselves operating enterprises outside of their accustomed milieu and homeland, particularly in ASEAN. In the business vernacular, the author describes their progress in adapting to the commercial practices of their new homes. The stories are related through studies in Comparative Management, spiced with some of the misconceptions and prejudices of earlier writers on the subject.

Readers who have neither interest in nor use for this academic vestibule can conveniently skip over Chapters I and III. The rest of the book is a fascinating revelation of the birth of the "Yellow Tide" in the business communities of Asia, with fine detail for the differences in the Philippines, Indonesia, Malaysia, Singapore, Thailand and Brunei. How these different beginnings and environments produced results that are strikingly similar is skillfully drawn by Dr. Victor S. Limlingan.

Dr. Limlingan is a man of varied academic interests, as evidenced by the range of academic degrees listed elsewhere in this book. This dexterity was also demonstrated in his career as a teacher in the Asian Institute of Management where he holds tenure as a full professor.

Originally assigned to Marketing subjects, Professor Limlingan extended his inquiries beyond the classroom and library. He first looked into the making and selling of local movies, and reached nickname familiarity with movie stars, directors and producers of the time.

Next he turned his curiosity to the newly evolving art of packaging. Printing methods and how they enhanced the packaging materials that sold otherwise mundane consumer products embellished his lecturettes. These supplemented his considerable teaching skills, a talent that became a near-legend in the Asian Institute of Management and an expertise that is difficult to master in programs that are almost entirely taught by the Case Method.

The printing of packaging materials is dominated by Chinese enterprises. Here he became acquainted with Chinese businessmen and became engrossed in studying the secrets of their success. This study resulted in three short monographs, one of which is *Chinese Pakulo Project Management in an Asian Setting*.

One short paper reveals the simplicity and effectiveness of the cash-flow accounting which most Chinese businessmen carry out mostly in their heads. Another runs through the psychological basis behind the involuted education of a business heir and successor.

Thus began the interest, and the effort, that culminated in this excellent and absorbing contribution to business literature on Overseas Chinese.

VICTOR A. LIM
November, 1987

CHAPTER I
THEMATIC FRAMEWORK

A. *Research Interest*

The focus of my research is on the Overseas Chinese in the ASEAN countries of Brunei, Indonesia, Malaysia, Philippines, Singapore and Thailand. (The most commonly used term for Chinese living abroad is *hua-ch'iao* or Overseas Chinese. The Chinese in Southeast Asia are called *Nanyang* [South Seas] *hua-ch'iao*) [1]. More specifically I am interested in the business strategies the Overseas Chinese pursued and the management practices they developed to achieve outstanding economic success in the ASEAN region.

My research interest in the Overseas Chinese in the ASEAN region is twofold. The first is fairly straightforward, documentation and quantification of this economic success story. My second and major interest is in formulating a conceptual framework for explaining this economic phenomenon. Moreover, while most observers of this success story have been more concerned with the **why,** I am more concerned with the **how.** I am less interested in the motivations that impelled the Overseas Chinese to business success; than in the mechanics of this accomplishment.

B. *The ASEAN Region*

ASEAN (Association of Southeast Asian Nations) was formed by Indonesia, Malaysia, Philippines, Singapore and Thailand in 1967. (Brunei Darussalam, a former British protectorate joined ASEAN shortly after attaining independence in January of 1984). Envisioned as a looser form of economic union than the European Economic Community, ASEAN has evolved into something more. Considerable progress has been achieved in forging a regional identity in terms of political cooperation, cultural and social interchange and economic coordination.

As a region, ASEAN boasts of a population (270 million in 1982) roughly equal to that of the EEC or the United States; of abundant natural resources (81.3 per cent of world rubber production, 64.2 per cent of world copra production, 62 per cent of world tin production, 33.8 per cent of world palm oil production and 21.6 per cent of world pineapple production); and of an impressive economic growth rate [2]. Table I-1 presents some selected statistics on the ASEAN countries.

The ASEAN countries as shown in the above statistics exhibit great diversity in land area, population sizes and per capita income.

Table I-1
Selected Statistics on the ASEAN Countries

Country	Land Area (000 km²)	Population (million)	GNP (US $M)	Per Capita (US $)
Brunei (1983)	5,765	0.2	3.73*	22,000
Indonesia (1982)	1,904,345	153.6	83.28	542
Malaysia (1983)	329,749	14.5	27.70	1,910
Philippines (1982)	300,000	50.7	36.49	720
Singapore (1983)	0.588	2.5	16.44	6,500
Thailand (1982)	514,000	50.0	34.86	697
Total	3,054,447	271.544	202.5	746

Sources: *The SGV Group: Doing Business in Indonesia 1985, The SGV Group: Doing Business in Malaysia 1983, The SGV Group: Doing Business in the Philippines 1983, The SGV Group: Doing Business in Thailand 1984, The Hongkong and Shanghai Banking Corporation Business Profile Series: Negara Brunei Darussalam,* December 1984, *The Hongkong and Shanghai Banking Corporation Business Profile Series: Republic of Singapore,* March 1985.
*Gross Domestic Product (GDP)

One of the things they do have in common is the presence of a distinct and economically successful minority, the Overseas Chinese[3].

C. *The Overseas Chinese in ASEAN*

The economic success of the Overseas Chinese in ASEAN has been observed by both journalists[4] and scholars[5]. This observation becomes more significant when we relate estimates of the percentage of Overseas Chinese to the total population of the ASEAN countries to the estimates of the share of the Overseas Chinese in the economic activities of these ASEAN countries.

On a worldwide basis, 96 per cent of all Overseas Chinese are in Southeast Asia (including Hong Kong and Macao) and 65 per cent of all Overseas Chinese are in the ASEAN countries[6]. Table I-2 presents an estimate of the population of Overseas Chinese in each of the ASEAN countries in 1974.

In contrast to the low percentage of the Overseas Chinese to the total population of the ASEAN countries are various estimates from different sources of their business and economic presence in the region.

The *Hua-ch'iao ching-chi nien-chien, 1974* [Overseas Chinese Economy Yearbook 1974] estimated that the Overseas Chinese in Thailand (8.5 per cent of the population) owned 90 per cent of all investments in the Commercial Sector, 90 per cent of all investments in the Manufacturing Sector and 50 per cent of all investments in the Banking and Finance Sector. Table I-3 presents the breakdown of the Overseas Chinese investment in Thailand.

Table I-2
Distribution of Overseas Chinese in the ASEAN Countries
1974

Country	Overseas Chinese* (Thousands)	Total Population (Millions)	Percentage of Overseas Chinese in Population
Brunei[b]	46.7	0.10	46.7 %
Indonesia	3,250.0	129.12	2.5
Malaysia[c]	3,687.0	10.38	35.5
Philippines	600.0	41.30	1.4
Singapore	1,579.9	2.22	72.0
Thailand	3,500.0	41.02	8.5
Total	12,663.6	224.14	5.6%

Sources: Yuan-li Wu and Chun-hsi Wu, *Economic Development in Southeast Asia: The Chinese Dimension*, page 133.
* As defined refers to permanent residents in the country (citizens and aliens alike) who consider themselves Chinese.
[b] Surprisingly Brunei has a larger percentage of Overseas Chinese in its population as compared to Malaysia. The oil revenues and the resulting per capita income of US$22,000 (higher than Japan's) have, however eased whatever tensions their economic success may have created.
[c] 1975 figures and for Peninsular Malaysia only.

Table I-3
Chinese Investment in Thailand
(1972)

Sector	Number of Firms	Capital (US $ Million)	Ethnic-Chinese Capital as Percentage of Total in Thailand
Commerce:			
Import and export	1,000	500.0	95
Wholesale and retail	5,000[c]	200.0	90
Restaurant	2,500	150.0	95
Service	500	100.0	80
Entertainment	150	50.0	70
Medicine	1,000	30.0	80
Other	500	5.0	90
Banking and finance	50	300.0	50
Manufacturing	2,000	300.0	90
Agriculture	100	0.5	2
Mining	50	2.0	30
Fishery	100	1.0	20
Total	12,960	1,640.5	

Source: *Hua-ch'iao ching-chi nien-chien* (Overseas Chinese Economy Yearbook), 1974, page 45.

In a research paper entitled, "Culture and Corporate Performance in the Philippines: The Chinese Puzzle," G. L. Hicks and S. G. Redding studied the largest 259 corporations out of the 1,000 largest corporations in the Philippines as listed in the 1980 Business Day Special Report. Hicks and Redding found that while the Overseas

Chinese constitute only 1.4 per cent of the population, 33.6 per cent of the top manufacturing firms were Chinese-owned and that 43.2 per cent of the top commercial firms were also Chinese-owned.

Table I-4 presents the breakdown of Overseas Chinese share in the top 259 Philippine corporations.

Table I-4
Chinese Firms in Top 259 Philippine Corporations
(1980)

Sector	Number of Chines Firms	Number of Firms	Chinese Firms/ Total Firms (%)
Commercial	32	74	43.2
Manufacturing	47	140	33.6
Mining	2	131	5.4
Services	1	14	1
Utilities	3	13	3.1
Agriculture	1	5	20.0
Total	86	259	33.2

Source: G. L. Hicks and S. G. Redding, "Culture and Corporate Performance in the Philippines: The Chinese Puzzle," in *Essays in Development Economics in Honor of Harry T. Oshima*, (Manila: Philippines Institute for Development Studies, 1982), Table 1, page 12.

In a research paper entitled, " The Ownership and Control of Large Corporations in Malaysia: The Role of the Chinese Business-man," Lim Mah Lui analyzed the composition of the directorships of the 100 largest corporations in Malaysia in 1974. Lim Mah Lui found that there were twice as many directors who were Malaysian Chinese (excluding the Singapore Chinese) as there were Malaysian Malays. Moreover, the Chinese directors were mainly "owner-directors" while the Malay directors were mainly "functional directors" representing the interests of state capital[7]. This disparity has resulted in a significant difference in the average income of the Malaysian Malay (*Bumiputra*) as compared to the Malaysian Chinese. Table I-5 presents the magnitude of such differences.

The *Hua-ch'iao ching-chi nien-chien, 1971* [Overseas Chinese Economy Yearbook 1971] estimated that in Indonesia, there were a total of 109,736 Chinese commercial establishments with an aggregate investment of US$765 million in 1959. It is estimated that this translates to over 50 per cent control of the wholesale and retail trade[8].

Finally in 1980, Yuan-li Wu and Chun-hsi Wu in their book, *Economic Development in Southeast Asia: The Chinese Dimension*, drew on previous estimates of the overseas Chinese investments and updated the figures for 1975. They then compared these figures with the direct investments of American, Japanese and other investor groups. Table I-6 presents their estimates.

Table I-5
Racial Mean Incomes in Peninsular Malaysia
(M $ per household per month)

Year	Chinese	Malay	Chinese/Malay
1957/58	300	139	2.158 x
1967/68	349	163	2.141
1970	399	177	2.254
1973	534	242	2.20
1976	787	345	2.281
1979	1,094	513	2.132

Sources: Household Budget Survey - Federation of Malaya 1957-58, SRM/Ford Social and Economic Survey 1967/68, Post Enumeration Survey of the 1970 population census, and *The Fourth Malaysia Plan 1981-1985*.

Table I-6
Estimated Investment of Selected Investor Groups in the ASEAN Countries
As of 1975
(US $ million)

Country	Overseas Chinese[a]	American[b]	Japanese[b]	Others[b]
Indonesia	1,638	959	2,095	1,994
Malaysia	1,943	n.a.	n.a.	n.a.
Philippines	931	217	118	158
Singapore	2,715	460	156	750
Thailand	2,689	27	78	82

Source: Yuan-li Wu and Chun-hsi Wu, *Economic Development in Southeast Asia: The Chinese Dimension* (Stanford: Hoover Institution Press, 1980), pages 34 and 170.
a "Overseas Chinese" refers to the Chinese (aliens and citizens alike) who reside permanently in the country. Investors from Hong Kong, Taiwan and the other ASEAN countries who may also be Chinese are included among the "Others."
b Since the figures on the American, Japanese and other investor groups represented officially declared investments with no adjustments to investments made prior to the establishment of investment boards and with no estimate of accumulated earnings, we used the *most conservative* estimates of the Overseas Chinese investment in each of the ASEAN countries.

The significant economic presence of the Overseas Chinese in the ASEAN countries was noted by earlier observers of the Overseas Chinese. In 1955, before government restrictions were imposed, Victor Purcell in his book, *The Chinese in Southeast Asia*, estimated that the Overseas Chinese owned 75 per cent of the rice mills in the Philippines and 80 to 90 per cent of the rice mills in Thailand. He further estimated that the Overseas Chinese conducted 70 per cent of all retail trade in Thailand and Indonesia, about 75 per cent in the Philippines and 85 per cent in Malaysia[9].

In 1959, Robert S. Elegant in his book, *The Dragon's Seed: Peking and the Overseas Chinese*, estimated that in the Philippines, the Overseas Chinese owned one-third of all retail establishments but do two-thirds of the business. He further estimated that in Malaya, the Overseas Chinese owned 35,000 out of a total of 47,000 retail establishments; 60,000 out of a total of 80,000 registered private firms. In the field of public transportation, the Overseas Chinese owned 80 per cent of the buses, 72 per cent of the freight trucks and 46 per cent of the taxis[10].

D. Explaining Away the Overseas Chinese Performance

Despite such statistics contrasting the small percentage of the Overseas Chinese population in ASEAN in relation to their economic presence in the region, alternative hypothesis of explaining away the statistics as due to other factors other than the racial one have been offerred.

One hypothesis that has been advanced would attribute the significant economic performance of the Overseas Chinese only to a small group of very wealthy businessmen within an otherwise economically normal Chinese community. The attribution of economic performance to a minority within a minority would of course still provide no explanation for the economic success of this more defined group. It would, however, lessen the sting of attributing such a performance to a racial factors.

Unfortunately the only statistics that we have come across concerning the distribution of income of the Overseas Chinese as compared to other racial groups indicated that the Chinese income distribution conformed more closely to the standard normal distribution than that of other racial groups. The *Mid-Term Review of the Second Malaysia Plan, 1971-1975* provided a breakdown of the income distribution of the Malay, Chinese and Indian households in Peninsular Malaysia.[11] This is shown on Table I-7.

Table I-7
Percentage Distribution of Households by Income and Race
in Peninsular Malaysia, 1970

Monthly Income Range (M$)	Malays	Chinese	Indians
$ 1–99	40.3 %	8.3 %	11.6%
$ 100–199	33.7	25.0	39.3
$ 200–399	18.3	38.0	31.3
$ 400–699	5.3	17.0	10.7
$ 700–1,499	2.0	9.2	5.3
$1,500–2,999	0.4	2.2	0.9
$3,000 or more	neg.	0.3	0.9

Source: *Mid-Term Review of the Second Malaysia Plan, 1971-1975* (Kuala Lumpur, Malaysia: Government Press, 1973), page 3.

One other hypothesis would seek to explain the economic performance of the Overseas Chinese in terms of external and extraneous factors rather than in terms of internal and intrinsic factors. For example, proponents of this hypothesis would explain the disparity in income between the Malaysian Chinese and the Malaysian Malay in terms of a difference in geographical distribution. This is usually illustrated by 1) citing the percentage of Urban Chinese (73.8 per cent of the total Chinese population in 1957) as contrasted to the Urban Malays (10.02 per cent in 1957); 2) citing the expected difference between over-all *urban* monthly income (M$319 in 1957/58) and the over-all *rural* monthly income (M$173 in 1957/58); and 3) using the above statistics to explain the difference between the average monthly income of the Malaysian Chinese (M$300 in 1957/58) and the average monthly income (M$139 in 1957/58) of the Malaysian Malays.

In 1984, we undertook a statistical analysis of this hypothesis with respect to the Malaysian experience. In that paper entitled, "The Income Equalization Program of the New Economic Policy of Malaysia: A Statistical Review," we presented the programs undertaken by the Malaysian government to attain income equalization among the races as well as a statistical review of the results.[12] A summary of our findings would be as follows:

1) The Malaysian government undertook several affirmative action programs which could be classified into three major categories: economic sector development; economic restructuring, and economic support.

2) In terms of economic sector development, these meant undertaking several development projects (i.e. Muda River Irrigation Project) aimed at increasing the income of the rural sector where most of the Malaysian Malays live.

3) In terms of economic restructuring, the Malaysian government initiated several programs aimed at achieving the following results:

   a) Increasing the percentage of Malays in the urban sector relative to the percentage of the Chinese;

   b) Increasing the percentage of Malays in the manufacturing or secondary sector relative to the percentage of the Chinese;

   c) Increasing the percentage of Malays in the service or tertiary sector relative to the percentage of the Chinese;

   d) Increasing the percentage of Malays in the higher income occupations relative to the percentage of the Chinese;

   e) Increasing Malay participation in terms of ownership of assets in the industrial and commercial sector relative to the percentage of the Chinese; and

   f) Increasing Malay ownership and control of the corporate sector relative to the Chinese.

4) In terms of economic support, the Malaysian government provided increased credit assistance, business consultancy services and training programs to the Malays.

5) The Malaysian government did achieve a significant number of its stated goals but the difference in income between the races persisted.
6) This led us to conclude that there was *no* statistical correlation between changes in these external factors (i.e. geographic dispersion, occupational distribution, etc.) and economic performance.

Returning to the example we cited above proposing geographical distribution to explain income disparity, we would note the following:

1) By 1980, the percentage of Urban Chinese had declined from a high of 73.48 per cent in 1957 to 54.00 per cent,
2) By 1980, the percentage of Urban Malays had increased from a low of 10.02 per cent in 1957 to 21.30 per cent,
3) By 1979, the ratio of urban to rural income had slightly increased from 1.84 times in 1957/58 to 1.90 times, and
4) By 1979, the ratio of Chinese to Malay income had barely decreased from 2.16 times in 1957/58 to 2.13 times.

Given the results of such a study, it is therefore quite difficult to explain the economic performance of the Overseas Chinese except in cultural and racial terms.

E. *Explaining the Overseas Chinese Performance: The Scholars*

The explanation for the remarkable business performance of the Overseas Chinese in the ASEAN countries has been attempted primarily by social scientists and politicians.

The historians have concentrated on recounting the remarkable saga of penniless immigrants transformed into wealthy merchants while the economists have focussed their research on the extent and depth of Overseas Chinese control of the economies of the ASEAN countries. Journalists, on the other hand have been content to simplistically attribute such success to strength of character [industry and frugality]; easier morals [corruption and bribery] or superior talent [a knack for business].

Understandably, the social scientists and the politicians have sought to explain the phenomenal business success of the Overseas Chinese in terms of their discipline or calling.

The psychologists, led by David McClelland[13], have sought to explain the success of the Overseas Chinese in terms of motivation. They note the high achievement drive (n-Ach) of immigrants and minority groups. Under this conceptual framework, the success of the Overseas Chinese could be explained under the following propositions:

1. McClelland suggests a high correlation between the motivation, need for achievement (n-Ach), and the inclination for entrepreneurship.
2. McClelland further suggests that those who emigrate also tend to have a high achievement drive. Thus the Chinese who migrated voluntarily from China to Southeast Asia would proportionately have more people with a high achievement drive than either the Chinese who chose not to migrate or the natives who chose to stay where they were.
3. Lastly, the high achievement drive of the Overseas Chinese who were a minority in the countries they settled in could only have entrepreneurship as an outlet for their high achievement drive.[14]

While the psychologists explanation is accepted by the sociologists as clarifying the motivations of immigrants and minority groups in tending towards entrepreneurial endeavors, they argue that such hypothesis does not completely explain why the Chinese migrants have been *more successful than other migrant groups* in the ASEAN countries.

Building on the explanation of the Overseas Chinese economic performance in terms of motivation, they have suggested an explanation similar to that proposed by Max Weber on the Protestant Work Ethic as the driving force behind the economic development of the West. In his book, *World Economic Development: 1979 and Beyond*, Herman Kahn argues that the Confucian Ethic which is characteristic of Japan, Korea, Taiwan, Hong Kong and Singapore explains much of the economic performance of these countries[15]. In their paper, "Culture, Causation and Chinese Management," S.G. Redding and G.L. Hicks extend the Confucian Hypothesis to the Overseas Chinese in Southeast Asia.[16]

Having accepted the Confucian or Chinese Culture hypothesis to explain the economic performance of the Overseas Chinese, the sociologists have set about trying to define what in sociological terms distinguishes the Overseas Chinese from other ethnic groups. Using their framework, the sociologists have defined the Overseas Chinese in terms of their cultural attributes and social organizations.[17]

But such a conceptual framework merely defines the context in which the Overseas Chinese achieved their business success. Linda Lim, summarizing the papers of several sociologists, concludes:

> Chinese social organization is neither necessary nor sufficient as an explanation of Chinese dominance or monopoly of particular lines of business in Southeast Asia.[18]

Interestingly, the sociological framework is used even by the few scholars in management interested in this area of research. For example, the Department of Management Studies of the University of Hong Kong has focussed on the role of Confucian Philosophy in the industrial development of East Asia (Singapore, Taiwan and Hong Kong) and on the Chinese management system.[19]

In summary therefore, explanations for the economic performance of the Overseas Chinese proposed by the scholars have focussed on motivations (entrepreneurial drive, work ethic, value system) rather than on mechanics.

Politicians, being more practical, have suggested how rather than why the Overseas Chinese have achieved economic success. Understandably, their explanation is articulated in political terms.

F. *Explaining Overseas Chinese Performance: The Politicians*

Due to political pressure, the politicians in the ASEAN countries have provided explanations for the Overseas Chinese phenomenon. While their explanations need not pass the rigorous scholarly standards of the social scientists, their explanations have had to show a modicum of logical consistency, as illustrated in this passage from the book of Victor Purcell, *The Chinese in Southeast Asia:*

> Pressed as to his case against the Chinese, the Filipino politician would say that the Chinese were too numerous, that they had more than half of the retail business in their hands, that they charge too high prices, cheated in weights and measures, and made high profits. Should it be objected that if this were so all the Filipino had to do was to open up a "tienda" [retail store] on his own and put the Chinese out of business in the village. The politician would probably shift his ground. He would now say that the Chinese standard of living is deplorably low; the owner of a Chinese tienda is willing to live in a small corner of his store, he eats almost nothing and works day and night, so does his family and his assistant as well if he has one. The Chinese in Manila, he says persistently disregard the eight-hour law. In fine, the charge now is that the Chinese runs his business with too little, not too great overhead expenses and profits. If this is true, then the Chinese gives excellent service to the Community as distributors. The Filipinos can buy cheaply because the Chinese live so meagerly[20].

One politician who has provided a historical, albeit politically-oriented explanation for the dominance of the Overseas Chinese in the economic activities of his country is the present Prime Minister of Malaysia, Mahathir bin Mohamad. In his book, *The Malay Dilemma,* Mahathir traces the economic history of the Malays during the different periods of Malaysian history to explain how dominance by the Chinese of the Malaysian economy occurred.

Mahathir starts by reminding us that there was a time in Malaysia's history without the ubiquitous Chinese shopkeeper.

Despite their absence during this period of Malaysian history, the Malay sultanates were already quite developed in commerce and industry. They had the facilities and the personnel to trade with the Indians and the Arabs who preceded the Chinese in Malaysia[21]. The Chinese came to Malaysia initially to trade, selling goods from China and buying local produce for export to China. Eventually, having ingratiated themselves with the ruling rajas, they settled down in increasing number and established a system of retail shops all over Malaysia.

The arrival of the Western colonizers merely strengthened the position of the Chinese traders. The Europeans who came primarily to trade and not to conquer immediately saw the usefulness of the Chinese traders:

> The Chinese knew the local language and had all the contacts as well as the set-up necessary to enable the European traders to milk the Malay sultanates dry. In no time at all, perfect "rapport" was established between the Chinese traders and the conquering merchants of the West. As this partnership grew and as the Chinese partners proved their usefulness over and over again, Chinese migration to Malaysia was encouraged and speeded up.[22]

By the time the Malays realized their economic dilemma, and by the time their political independence placed them in a position to do something, the situation was too difficult to change:

> Chinese business methods and the extent of their control of the economy is such that competition between their community and other communities is quite impossible. Their close-knit communal business tie-ups and connections, their extensive hold over the wholesale and retail business, their control of transportation, their powerful banks and their own wealth are such as to constitute an impregnable barrier against any substantial encroachment by other communities in their economic preserves in a free enterprise society.[23]

It is a matter of supreme irony that the Overseas Chinese, the most practical of people, should attract primarily the interest of scholars and that this most apolitical of minorities in the region should have its behavior explained in political terms.

The objective of this book is to present *an alternative framework* for explaining the success of the Overseas Chinese in the ASEAN region. Such a framework would seek to explain the success of the Overseas Chinese in business and management terms. However, I do *not* propose to adopt the standard approach used by management scholars in explaining non-Western business and management systems.

G. The Comparative Management Approach

Management scholars, in seeking to explain management practices different from the Western model, have used what has come to be known as the Comparative Management Approach.

Negandhi and Prasad, in their book, *Comparative Management*, undertook a survey of the management practices and effectiveness of ninety two (92) industrial firms in five developing countries (Argentina, Brazil, Philippines, India and Uruguay).[24] Of these 92 firms, 47 were American subsidiaries and 45 were local firms comparable to those subsidiaries. Comparability between the American firms and the local firms was established on the basis of industry, technology, market conditions and size of work force. The authors then sought to compare the American managerial system with the managerial systems from the developing countries on the bases of management processes and practices and management effectiveness. Management processes and practices were identified as planning for the future, building the organization, policy making, leadership, motivation and control mechanisms. Management effectiveness was divided into three measures of effectiveness: over-all effectiveness, effectiveness at the manager level and effectiveness at the worker level. As designed, the survey sought to establish relationships between management effectiveness (the dependent variable) and the different management processes and practices. In general, the study concluded that while there is considerable impact from environmental factors on management effectiveness, the management practices concerning planning, organizing, staffing and controlling were not unduly restricted by environmental and cultural factors.

Another comparative management study reached different conclusions. Geert Hofstede during a period of eleven years (1967-1978) conducted research on the work-related values of over 116,000 employees ranging from unskilled workers to research scientists across 50 countries of a large multinational corporation.[25] Using four independent criteria—individualism versus collectivism, large or small power distance, strong or weak uncertainty avoidance, and masculinity versus femininity—Hofstede found remarkable and stable differences between countries despite the fact that the respondents were working under the same corporate culture. Thus, while the sample was biased in terms of being non-representative of the country from which the respondents were drawn, Hofstede could argue that a more representative sample would merely prove his conclusions more strongly.

From such findings, Hofstede argued against the convergence theory of management, pointing out how culture-bound management is.

Were I to adopt such a comparative management approach, my research effort would concentrate on documenting Chinese management practices, organizing such practices into some management framework and then comparing such practices with the Western management model.

Management scholars at the Centre of Asian Studies at the University of Hong Kong have adopted such an approach. As such, their research has tended to focus on *what* makes Chinese managers and Chinese management different from their Western counterparts. For example, the Centre has published several studies on how Chinese managers perceive reality differently from Western managers. Another paper deals with the role of face in the organizational perceptions of managers.[26]

While such studies are quite useful, and I propose to use them in my research, I hold the view that comparative management analysis of the Chinese vis-a-vis Western management can be undertaken *only after* the Chinese managerial system has been explained on its own terms.

As an argument for such an approach, I refer to the initial studies on the Japanese managerial system. Being initially compared to the Western management system, it was judged by Western standards and thus judged quite adversely. For example, a paper published in the March 1964 issue of the *Academy of Management Journal* began:

> Americans who look at the organization and practice of Japanese Management always have the same initial reaction: can this really work?
> There is little formal organization, less delegation of authority and little reliance on staff work even in the largest firms.[27]

This initial reaction to the Japanese managerial system is echoed in an article on the Chinese managerial system. The article in the July 1978 issue of *Management Today* concluded that:

> Perhaps, the most serious disadvantage of the traditional Chinese management system is that even within the small hierarchy, there is virtually no delegation. Normally the family with the most wealth has the most say, and the Western idea of delegated responsibility is only slowly being accepted. All decisions are passed up the line to the boss. The underlings, therefore have little opportunity to gain experience in decision-making or to take steps they can see to be necessary.[28]

Even in instances where the Japanese management system was judged to be both different and effective, there was still the tendency to use the Japanese managerial system to validate universal management principles or to explain why the management principles were still valid despite the seeming Japanese exception.

Richard D. Robinson, in his 1964 book, *International Business Policy*, noted:

A further problem challenging some of the more thoughtful members of the international business community is the suspicion that certain values long held at least in verbal awe in professional management circles may not be universally valid. The concept of complete neutrality in interpersonal relations may not, after all be conducive to the most effective communication within a large organization. The Japanese experience would indicate that at least some modification of the neutral and achievement norms may generate greater efficiency, at least under some circumstances and in some cultures . . . The point is that the greater ease of effective communication within the more affective and group-oriented Japanese structure may more than offset the technical inefficiency of not necessarily maximizing the productivi*ty* of individuals by impersonally matching ability and challenge.

Only when Yoshino in his book, *Japan's Managerial System: Tradition and Innovation*, explained the Japanese Managerial System on its own terms was a more accurate picture of the Japanese Management System presented.[30] Moreover, subsequent comparisons with other managerial systems became more balanced and meaningful.

Another reason for *not* adopting the comparative management approach is the type of research I propose to undertake. Scholarly work can be described as a continuous cycle of gathering data to provide the basis for models and theorems and of formulating theorems and models to explain newly generated data. I propose to concentrate on the model- or theorem-formulating cycle. I consider the comparative management approach to be more appropiate in the data-gathering cycle.

H.Hypothesis Formulation

Under the theorem-formulating process, I would choose a dependent variable, identify the independent variables and then seek to identify as precisely as possible the relationship between the independent variables and the dependent variables.

Within this framework, I would choose the performance of the Overseas Chinese in the ASEAN countries as the dependent variable. In my review of the explanations offered by the scholars and politicians I we have generated three possible independent variables; value systems (Chinese and/or migrant), social systems (Chinese social organizations) and technology (Mahathir's view that the Chinese had the skills which the natives could not or would not develop). To generate additional independent variables and to validate all the independent variables I propose to resort to historical analysis. I expect a review of the history of the Overseas Chinese in the ASEAN countries to be the basis for identifying and validating the independent variables.

To define the relationship between the dependent variable and the independent variables, I shall propose a model which I have termed the Business Policy model. The Business Policy model postulates that the relationship between the dependent variable and the independent variable is explained by the formulation (or more likely, the discovery) of a business strategy by the Overseas Chinese which is appropiate to the independent variables, and the development of management practices which follow from the appropriate business strategy and which are consistent with the independent variables. The Business Policy model further postulates that the most appropriate strategy and structure would result in a higher value of the dependent variable.

I propose to adopt the Business Policy model by postulating the existence of a Chinese business organization. Using the Business Policy model, I shall further define the specific business strategies and management practices and test their validity in the case histories of specific firms and in the business statistics and studies generated on Chinese firms.

I mentioned earlier that the standard approach to research efforts on non-Western business systems is the comparative management analysis approach. However, two related research efforts have followed the alternative approach we propose to pursue.

In his 1970 Harvard DBA thesis, entitled, "The Strategies of Chinese Enterprises in Hong Kong," John Espy formulated and provided evidence for his thesis that there was a correlation between corporate strategy and corporate performance. More specifically, his survey of several high-growth Hong Kong companies indicated that they pursued a strategy which focussed on the Western European or American markets rather than on the Hong Kong or Southeast Asian markets, choosing labor-intensive, low-technology, mature industries to take full advantage of Hong Kong's comparative advantage in labor costs, and competing with other Hong Kong companies on the basis of the ability to accept large orders and reliability in terms of meeting quality standards and meeting delivery commitments. This strategy has resulted in their superior performance.[31]

In his book, *Third World Multinationals: The Rise of Foreign Investment from Developing Countries*, Louis T. Wells, Jr. did *not* follow the comparative management analysis research approach (comparing the differences between Developed Country and Developing Country Multinationals) or even the neoclassical economic models as the basis for his research effort.

The need for diversification explains some of the actions of foreign investors from developing countries, but most of this study relies on three sets of concepts that are quite different from neoclassical theory. They have proved particularly useful in understanding multinationals from the United States, Europe and Japan. The concepts are based on the assumption that certain firms have skills and information that are not easily available to others; that managers are risk-averse, face costs in acquiring information about alternatives, and as a result are likely to select alternatives that satisfy their goals rather than maximize profits; and that certain kinds of transactions can be more effectively conducted within the same firm than between two unrelated firms.[32]

I now turn to the data base on which I expect to formulate and validate my hypothesis.

I. *The Data Base*

The data base on the Overseas Chinese in East and Southeast Asia is best summed up by G. L. Hicks and S. G. Redding in their paper entitled, "Uncovering Sources of East Asian Economic Growth":

One is struck now by the very large volume of research on the Japanese economy and its form of organization. Equally striking is the almost complete lack of work on the overseas Chinese or Korean equivalent. This latter problem is partially counter-balanced by a large and varied literature on East Asia in anthropology, sociology, political science, history and economic geography, the sifting of which can often allow the reconstruction of an explanation of managerial and/or economic behavior. Even here there remains little of such work, gathering together disciplines and using the secondary sources.[33]

Given this situation, I propose to use the data generated by the other disciplines to develop a detailed description of the Overseas Chinese phenomenon. More specifically:
1. I shall draw on historical sources to describe the movement of the Overseas Chinese into the ASEAN countries, the historical backdrop under which this occurred, and the responses their presence and economic dominance have elicited from the various ASEAN governments. Examples of such historical sources are:
   a. Victor Purcell, *The Chinese in Southeast Asia*
   b. Lois Mitchison, *The Overseas Chinese: A Background Book*
   c. Mary F. Sommers Heidhues, *Southeast Asia's Chinese Minorities*

d. Victor Purcell, *The Chinese in Malaya*
e. G. William Skinner, *Chinese History in Thailand: An Analytical History*
f. R. J. Coughlin, *Double Identity: The Chinese in Modern Thailand*
g. G. William Skinner, *The Chinese Minority (in Indonesia)*
h. Edgar Wickberg, *The Chinese in Philippine Life: 1850-1898*

2. I shall draw from economic sources, a quantitative, sectoral and time-series description of the magnitude and range of the economic performance of the Overseas Chinese. In addition to tapping the standard sources from the ASEAN governments, I shall use data generated by the Overseas Chinese Affairs Commission (OCAC) of the Republic of China (Taiwan) as well as by various Overseas Chinese associations.

3. I shall draw from the journalistic sources, the more specific and more colorful description of outstanding members and companies among the Overseas Chinese.

4. I shall draw from the scholarly researches of the sociologists' precise definitions of the culture, organization and social practices of the Overseas Chinese. Examples of such researches are:
a. Maurice Freedman, *The Study of Chinese Society*
b. W. E. Willmott, *Economic Organization in Chinese Society*
c. John T. Omohundro, *The Chinese in Iloilo: Kin and Commerce in a Central Philippine City.*

5. I shall also draw from the scholarly papers of sociologists' case studies describing specific business practices and activities of the Overseas Chinese. Examples of such papers are:
a. Clifton A. Barton, "Trust and Credit: Some Observations Regarding Business Strategies of Overseas Chinese Traders in South Vietnam"
b. S. Stanley Eitzen, "Two Minorities: The Jews of Poland and the Chinese of the Philippines"
c. L. A. Peter Gosling, "Chinese Crop Dealers in Malaysia and Thailand: The Myth of the Merciless Monopsonistic Middleman"
d. James A. Hafner, "Market Gardening in Thailand: The Origins of an Ethnic Chinese Monopoly"
e. Donald M. Nonini, "The Chinese Truck Transport "Industry" of a Peninsular Malaysia Market Town"
f. Aram A. Yengoyan, "The Buying of Futures: Chinese Merchants and the Fishing Industry in Capiz, Philippines"

To this secondary data, I propose to add previous research work I have undertaken on the business strategies and management practices of the Overseas Chinese. Specifically I refer to the notes on Chinese management I wrote as a member of the faculty of the Asian Institute of Management:

a. "The Chinese 'Pakulo': Project Management in an Asian Setting"
b. "The Chinese Walkabout: A Case Study in Entrepreneurial Education"
c. "The Chinese Trading Company: An Organization for Opportunity Exploration and Exploitation"

I shall also be drawing on the data and analyses of the papers I have written as a doctoral student at the Harvard Business School:

a. "The Income Equalization Program of the New Economic Policy of Malaysia: A Statistical Review"
b. "The Coming of Managerial Capitalism in Malaysia"
c. "The Visible Hand in Southeast Asia"
d. "Professional Management in Developing Countries"

Lastly, during a research trip to the ASEAN countries in 1984, I conducted interviews with several Chinese businessmen, several partners of a consulting company engaged in providing consultancy services to Chinese businessmen, several non-Chinese businessmen and some experts on management in Southeast Asia. Table I-8 presents a breakdown of the people I have interviewed.

Table I-8
1984 Research Trip to Southeast Asia

Category	Chinese[a]	SGV[b]	Institutes[c]	Total
Indonesia	2	2	4	8
Malaysia	3	1	2	6
Philippines	2	1	2	5
Singapore	1	0	1	2
Thailand	2	2	1	5
Total	**10**	**6**	**10**	**26**

[a] Interview with Chinese businessman or his senior manager
[b] SyCip, Gorres, Velayo & Company, a Philippine-based consulting firm with offices in the ASEAN region. Number indicates interview with partner.
[c] Interview with management institutes (i.e. Lembaga Pengembangan Perbankan Indonesia) and management associations (i.e. Thailand Management Association) in the region.

J. Objectives And Research Guidelines

My objective therefore, is the formulation of a business policy model by which the economic success of the Overseas Chinese can be explained, analyzed and synthesized. More specifically, I propose the division of this overall objective into the following sub-objectives:

1. To explain how the business strategies and management practices of the successful Overseas Chinese firms have been based on an effective fit between the economic environment they operate in and the "corporate culture" that they have adopted from their own distinct Chinese culture.

2. To relate the distinct business strategy and management practices of the Overseas Chinese to the Western Model, the Japanese Model and to other models of management within the framework of Comparative Management Analysis.
3. To provide an effective basis for public policy formulation by the public policy makers in ASEAN.

Based on these objectives, I propose to follow these research guidelines:

1. The litmus test of my research effort is the capability of my model to explain the existing data on the Overseas Chinese in Southeast Asia more consistently than any alternative model.
2. The validity and reliability of the data which I will use, being secondary rather than primary shall be assured through the use of a multi-disciplinary approach. Initially, I have pinpointed these approaches: historical, economic, statistical, case studies, journals and publications, in-depth interviews with management consultants dealing with the Overseas Chinese as clients and with some Overseas Chinese businessmen.
3. The basic model I propose to build on will be the business policy model. I propose to view the Overseas Chinese as formulating and pursuing business strategies based on the environment they operate in, on the values they cherish, and the opportunities they perceive.
4. In terms of highlighting the distinctive corporate strategies of the Overseas Chinese, I shall use the comparative management analysis approach by comparing the Overseas Chinese in Asian vis-a-vis Western companies, Japanese companies, and Hong Kong or Taiwanese companies. In addition, I shall use the ASEAN countries as defining the range and scope of the business strategies of the Overseas Chinese.
5. I propose to focus on a specific organization which best exemplifies the distinctive management style of the Overseas Chinese in much the same way that researchers have focussed on the multidivisional, integrated companies such as the oil companies and on the Japanese trading company. My company focus shall be the Chinese trading company.

K. *Significance of the Research*

It is my hope that the findings and conclusions in this book will be of some significance to the following sectors of management practitioners and scholars:

1. For Southeast Asian and developing country managers, a possible model managerial system more suitable to their environment and a corporate culture more familiar to them. At the very

least, I expect my book to encourage them to develop their own distinct managerial system.

2. For Southeast Asian public managers, an alternative method of assessing the impact and effectiveness of their public policies with respect to the private sector. At the very least, I expect this book to caution public policy makers to formulate public policies on the basis of a realistic assessment of the operations of the Overseas Chinese firms.

3. For scholars interested in comparative management analysis, I hope to present a description of a managerial system which would enable them to compare with the American, European and Japanese managerial systems. I expect to stimulate interest in comparative management analysis between the managerial systems of developing countries as compared to developed countries.

NOTES

1. Exactly who should be considered a *hua-ch'iao* has given rise to four different views. The first rests on the literal meaning of the two words: *hua* means a Chinese, whereas *ch'iao* means a short stay as a visitor. By this definition, all Chinese living outside China on a short-term basis should be regarded as Overseas Chinese. A second interpretation is based on the simple fact of overseas residence and Chinese citizenship. Both those who have emigrated from China to foreign countries and their offspring born and brought up in those countries qualify. The third definition reflects a legal point of view. There are two versions. In the first, all Chinese who have emigrated to, or are residents of, foreign countries and who have not lost their Chinese citizenship are regarded as Overseas Chinese. In the second, all persons who have emigrated from China and their offspring are considered Overseas Chinese even if they have acquired foreign citizenship. The fourth interpretation would consider all persons who regard themselves as Chinese irrespective of their national status or their ability to speak the Chinese language as *hua ch'iao* (excerpted from Yuan-li Wu and Chun-hsi Wu, *Economic Development in Southeast Asia: the Chinese Dimension* (Stanford: Hoover Institution Press, 1980), page 118. In this book, we shall adopt the fourth interpretation: the Overseas Chinese in ASEAN are those persons residing in the ASEAN countries who regard themselves as Chinese.

2. For more information on ASEAN and the ASEAN countries, see Thomas W. Allen, *The ASEAN Report* (Hong Kong: Dow Jones Publishing Company (Asia), Inc., 1979) and Brian Wawn, *The Economies of the Asean Countries: Indonesia, Malaysia, Philippines, Singapore and Thailand* (New York: St. Martin's Press, 1982).

3. The other significant minority in the region are the Overseas Indians. While having made significant strides as immigrants, they have not been as economically successful as the Chinese. For a description of their economic achievements, see Virginia Thompson and Richard Adloff, *Minority Problems in Southeast Asia* (Stanford: Stanford University Press, 1955), pp. 59-134.

4. Louis Kraar, "The Wealth and Power of the Overseas Chinese," *Fortune*, March 1971; "The Silent Spread of Chinese Business in Southeast Asia," *Asian Finance*, June 15, 1977; and D. Jenkins, "Traders Who Came to Stay," *Far East Economic Review*, September 21, 1979.

5. Yuan-li Wu and Chun-hsi Wu, *Economic Development in Southeast Asia: The Chinese Dimension* (Stanford: Hoover Institution Press, 1980), and Linda Y. C. Lim and L. A. Peter Gosling, *The Chinese in Southeast Asia: Ethnicity and Economic Activity* (Singapore: Maruzen Asia, 1983).

6. Sen-Dou Chang, "The Distribution and Occupations of Overseas Chinese," *Geographical Review*, January 1968, p. 99.

7. Mah Hui Lim, "The Ownership and Control of Large Corporations in Malaysia: The Role of Chinese Businessmen," in Linda Y. C. Lim and L. A. Peter Gosling, *The Chinese in Southeast Asia: Ethnicity and Economic Activity* (Singapore: Maruzen Asia, 1983).

8. Yuan-li Wu and Chun-hsi Wu, *Economic Development in Southeast Asia: The Chinese Dimension* (Stanford: Hoover Institution Press, 1980), p. 63. Wu and Wu (page 30) cite Louis Kraar for their estimate of Chinese control of the wholesale and retail trade.

9. Victor Purcell, *The Chinese in Southeast Asia* (London: Oxford University Press, 1980), pp. 83, 130, and 547.

10. Robert S. Elegant, *The Dragon's Seed: Peking and the Overseas Chinese* (New York: St. Martin's Press, 1959), p. 82.

11. *Mid-Term Review of the Second Malaysia Plan, 1971-1975* (Kuala Lumpur, Malaysia: Government Press, 1973, p. 3. While the Malaysian government issued two additional five year plans, *The Third Malaysia Plan, 1976-1980* and *The Fourth Malaysia Plan,1981-1985*, statistics on income distribution among the races were discontinued.

12. Victor S. Limlingan, "The Income Equalization Program of the New Economic Policy of Malaysia: A Statistical Review," unpublished mimeograph, 1985.

13. David McClelland, *The Achieving Society* (Princeton: Van Nostrand, 1961). Interestingly, McClelland never cites the Overseas Chinese as one of the examples of an achieving society.

14. For studies on the linkage between entrepreneurship and minority groups, see Everett Hagen, *On the Theory of Social Change: How Economic Growth Begins* (Homewood, Illinois: Richard Dorsey, 1962) and Peter Kilby, *Entrepreneurship and Economic Development* (New York: Free Press, 1971).

15. Herman Kahn, *World Economic Development: 1979 and Beyond* (Boulder, Colorado: Westview Press, 1979). See also R. MacFarquhar, "The Post-Confucian Challenge," *The Economist*, Febuary 9, 1980, pp. 67-72.

16. S. G. Redding and G. L. Hicks, "Culture, Causation and Chinese Management," Working Paper, Centre of Asian Studies, University of Hong Kong, 1983.

17. See Chapter six, The Chinese Managerial System, for a more detailed discussion of Chinese culture and its relationship to the Chinese Managerial System

18. Linda Y. C. Lim and L. A. Peter Gosling, *The Chinese in Southeast Asia: Ethnicity and Economic Activity* (Singapore: Maruzen Asia, 1983), p. 5-6.

19. G. L. Hicks and S. G. Redding, "Industrial East Asia and the Post-Confucian Hypothesis: A Challenge to Economics," Working Paper, Centre of Asian Studies, University of Hong Kong, 1983, and S. G. Redding and G. L. Hicks, "Culture, Causation and Chinese Management," Working Paper, Centre of Asian Studies, University of Hong Kong, 1983.

20. Victor Purcell, *The Chinese in Southeast Asia* (London: Oxford University Press, 1980), p. 546.

21. Mahathir bin Mohamad, *The Malay Dilemma*, (Singapore: Times Books International, 1970), pp. 32-33.

22. Ibid., p. 35.

23. Ibid., p. 54.

24. Anant R. Negandhi and S. Benjamin Prasad, *Comparative Management* (New York: Appleton-Century-Crofts, 1971). For other and earlier comparative management analysis studies, see Frederick Harbison and Charles Myers, *Management in the International World: An International Analysis* (New York: McGraw-Hill Book Company, Inc., 1959); R. N. Farmer and B. M. Richman, *Comparative Management and Economic Progress* (Homewood, Illinois: Richard D. Irwin, 1965); and Stanley Davis, *Comparative Management: Cultural and Organizational Perspectives* (Englewood Cliffs, New Jersey: Prentice-Hall, 1971). For a more recent review on the status of research on Comparative Management, see the Fall 1983 issue of the *Journal of International Business Studies*.

25. Geert Hofstede, "The Cultural Relativity of Organizational Practices and Theories," *Journal of International Business Studies*, Fall 1983.

26. This focus on culture has resulted in very specific studies on how Chinese managers perceive reality differently; see S. G. Redding Cognition as an Aspect of Culture and Its Relation to the Management Process: An Exploratory View of the Chinese Case," *Journal of Management Studies*, Vol. 17 No. 2, 1980 and S. G. Redding and M. Ng, "The Role of Face

in the Organizational Perceptions of Chinese Managers, " *Organizational Studies*, Vol. 3 No. 3, 1982.

27. Joseph N. Froomkin, "Management and Organization in Japanese Industry," *Academy of Management Journal*, March 1964. The article was featured in two books on International Management; in Dalton E. McFarland, *Current Issues and Emerging Concepts in Management* (Boston: Houghton Miflin Company, 1966) and in Benjamin S. Prasad, *Management in International Perspective* (New York: Appleton-Century-Crofts, 1967).

28. Tom Lester, "Hong Kong's Management Mix," *Management Today*, July 1978, pp. 80-89.

29. Richard D. Robinson, *International Business Policy* (New York: Holt, Rinehart and Winston, 1964), pp. 138-139.

30 Michael Y. Yoshino, *Japan's Managerial System: Tradition and Innovation* (Cambridge: The Massachusetts Institute of Technology Press, 1968).

31. John Lee Espy, "The Strategies of Chinese Enterprises in Hong Kong," Harvard Business School, Unpublished DBA Thesis, June 1970.

32. Louis T. Wells, Jr., *Third World Multinationals: The Rise of Foreign Investment from Developing Countries* (Cambridge: Massachusetts Institute of Technology Press, 1983), pp. 13-14.

33. Hicks and Redding, "Uncovering Sources of East Asian Economic Growth," Working Paper, Centre of Asian Studies, Universityof Hong Kong, 1983, p. 18.

CHAPTER II
THE HISTORY OF THE OVERSEAS CHINESE
IN THE ASEAN REGION

A. *The Dragon's Seed: The Traders*

The view espoused by politicians[1] and journalists[2] that the Chinese came to the ASEAN countries as traders and decided to stay and do business in the host country is valid *only* for a small group of the Overseas Chinese who came to the area at an early period (1300-1870 A.D.). The later (1870-1940 A.D.), much larger group of Chinese immigrants were of humbler origins.

The earliest indicators of contact between Imperial China and the pre-colonial states of what are now the ASEAN countries go back to the third and even fourth century B.C. (Han Dynasty) as suggested by the archaeological finds of Chinese artifacts (porcelain pots and carved jade trinkets) in Malaya (present-day Malaysia and Singapore), Sumatra, Java, and Borneo (present-day East Malaysia, Brunei, and Indonesia). Anthropologists, studying the succeeding periods (the Southern Sung Dynasty) have noted traces of Chinese influence in terms of technology (the potter's wheel), language (absorption of Chinese words into the dialect) and ideas (politics and religion).

Chinese historical records which were more detailed than those from the ASEAN countries trace the development of contacts as initiated by diplomatic missions which progressed into trading expeditions and eventually into establishment of trading relations.[3]

Thus in 607 A.D., Emperor Sui Yang-ti of China sent a mission by sea to Siam (present-day Thailand) to establish commercial relations with that kingdom. Between 756 and 779 A.D., three envoys from Java (now Indonesia) arrived at the court of the Emperor of China bearing gifts. In 977 A.D., Arabs came to the Chinese court as envoys from the king of Brunei. In 1378 A.D., the king of Pahang (now Malaysia) sent envoys with letters and tribute to China. In 1405 A.D., the Emperor Yung Lo sent a delegate to Luzon (now the Philippines) to exercise sovereignty over the area.[4]

All these developments must be placed in the greater context of the more pervasive influence of the Arabs, the Persians and the Indians. The Chinese, given their sense of national sufficiency and the feeling that nothing of great value could be obtained from the kingdoms of the Southern Seas (present-day Southeast Asia), ceded the area to the Arabs, the Persians and the Indians. In addition to establishing a strong trading presence in the area, they would bring the more enduring presence of their religions, Buddhism, Hinduism, and Islam. In fact the presence and possible importance of

Southeast Asia to Imperial China was most probably reported by Chinese Buddhist monks on a pilgrimage to India via the Southern Seas.[5]

In any case, by the time the Europeans arrived in the area (the Portuguese in 1518, the Spaniards in 1565, the Dutch in 1598, and the British in 1612), the Chinese traders were a presence though not a dominant one in the region.[6]

The prevailing belief has been that the European colonizers saw the value of the Chinese traders as the ideal vehicles for exploiting the natives and thus encouraged their migration into the colonies. Except in the isolated case of the use of the Chinese to collect taxes in Indonesia[7], the European powers barely tolerated the Chinese traders. The Chinese they eventually allowed into the colonies in the high noon of their colonial rule (1870-1930 A.D.) were not the Chinese traders but the Chinese laborers (coolie labor). It is from these lowly Chinese laborers that the present-day army of Overseas Chinese merchants and entrepreneurs sprang.

That this is a more accurate version of the origins of the Overseas Chinese is argued by several prominent historians.

Victor Purcell begins the introduction to his seminal book, *The Chinese in Southeast Asia*, with these words:

> The Overseas Chinese in Southeast Asia, during their history covering some 600 years, have passed through a number of distinct phases. The first was when these countries were still ruled by their native princes and the Chinese settlements were small... The second phase was when the European powers had established their colonies, and the improved trade opportunities as well as the protection encouraged them to immigrate into them in larger numbers. But it was only in the great period of European colonial expansion in the last quarter of the nineteenth century and onwards, when this immigration increased to a flood to meet the demand for manpower created by the 'opening up' process that the third phase was inaugurated.[8]

David Joel Steinberg et al., in their book, *In Search of Southeast Asia*, make the same point:

> In a few places, Chinese settled down as peasants . . . Some came as merchants from the beginning, simply moving outward along their commercial channels from China coast cities. But the great majority came, packed in the steerage of the coolie ships, as simple laborers, owing passage money to those for whom they first worked. They came to work on the European plantations of Sumatra's East Coast Residency, to build the 2,000 miles of Thai railways, to work the tin deposits of Southern Thailand, Malaya, Bangka and Billiton, and to work in a variety of new jobs in the port cities and towns of Southeast

Asia, as labor for the docks, hand sawmills, rice mills and the building trades.[9]

Lennox A. Mills concurs with the other historians in his chapter on the Chinese in his book, *Southeast Asia: Illusion and Reality in Politics and Economics:*

China's trade with Southeast Asia has gone on for two thousand years or more. There were groups of merchants in the principal seaports, but the Chinese did not settle abroad in large numbers until the establishment of European rule had created stable conditions. From the nineteenth century onwards the majority of the immigrants were manual laborers and peasants, but they were unwilling to follow their former occupations when they reached Southeast Asia, preferring more lucrative forms of employment. Moreover, in some countries local laws prevented them from being rice farmers. They were exclusively interested in making a living and saving enough to return home as soon as possible; and they took very little interest in local politics. It has been said that the Westerners colonized the tropics by exporting capital and establishing estates, mines and commercial enterprises, while Chinese colonization relied on brains and brawn. The typical Chinese immigrant was a penniless laborer who worked with concentrated energy until he had saved enough to forsake manual labor for some form of business. Gradually he rose in the economic scale, and he might end as a wealthy merchant, estate-, mine, or ship-owner, or banker. If Horatio Alger had chosen to place his success stories among Chinese rather than Americans, he could have found a plethora of examples for his favorite theme of poor boy from the farm makes good in the big cities.[10]

Prior to the industrial revolution in Europe and the transformation of the economies of the ASEAN countries into the "plantation or culture" economies, Europeans came to the Far East principally to trade (i.e. the Dutch East India Company rather than the Dutch government) for cloves, pepper, nutmegs, and other spices.[11] Their attitude towards the Chinese was ambivalent. On the one hand, the Chinese were sources for the other products that Europe needed, such as silk, tea, woven cotton, ink, paper, etc. On the other hand, the Chinese were competitors for the products from the Far East.[12]

The Europeans sought to restrict the Chinese to mere suppliers of Chinese goods by imposing a monopoly on the exportation of spices, sugar, tobacco, and other goods produced in the colonies under their control, by restricting the Chinese to the principal trading posts, and by controlling the size of the Chinese population through strict immigration rules. When all else failed, massacres were even resorted to.[13]

Thus when the Chinese population in Batavia (present-day Jakarta, Indonesia) grew from about 400 in 1619 to over 10,000 in 1725 despite attempts to limit immigration, the Dutch East India Company decided to clear Batavia of the Chinese. In the Massacre of 1740 that resulted from such an attempt to reduce the Chinese population, over 10,000 Chinese were killed. This unplanned massacre by the Dutch effectively reduced the population to about 3,500.

In the other islands of Indonesia, Dutch policy was no less severe. In fact the Dutch could be held responsible for the decimation of the only large-scale Chinese settlement in the ASEAN countries prior to the large-scale importation of Chinese labor from the 1850's to the 1930's.

From 1772 onwards the Chinese settled in West Borneo for the purpose of gold mining. Organized into business groupings called *kongsis*, the Chinese grew numerous and powerful enough to disregard the sovereignty of the ruling sultans. By 1823, when the Dutch bought the mining concessions from the sultans, the Chinese numbered about 150,000 out of a total estimated population of 450,000. In the ensuing bitter clashes, the Dutch took control of the trading ports and began a systematic campaign to exercise control over what became Dutch Borneo (present-day Kalimantan, Indonesia). By 1880, prior to the reversal of Dutch policy on Chinese migration, the Chinese population in Dutch Borneo was down 28,000 as a result of massacres and emigration.[14]

The Spaniards in the Philippines followed basically the same approach. The Chinese were restricted to Manila and to an area called the *Parian*, outside the walled city (Intramuros) of Manila. Again, when the Chinese population rose from 2,000 in 1591 to over 15,000 in 1600, attempts to control their size resulted in the Massacre of 1603. About 15,000 Chinese were killed. This effectively reduced the population to about 500. In 1606, to prevent the recurrence of such a tragedy, the Spaniards limited by decree the size of the Chinese to at most 6,000. However, either through Spanish ineptitude or Chinese ignorance, the population by 1638 was again 25-30,000. In the second Massacre of 1639, an estimated 22-24,000 Chinese were killed. This effectively reduced the population to below the maximum of 6,000. The decree was then strictly implemented such that 200 years later in 1847, the size of the Chinese population was still below 6,000.[15]

The very limited scale of trading operation carried on by the European colonizers did not require a substantial Chinese population. For example, the British, who actively encouraged the migration of the Chinese into the Straits Settlements (Malacca, Penang and Singapore), did not really have sizeable Chinese populations. Table II-1 presents the Chinese population in the Straits Settlements prior to the economic transformation.

Table II-1
Chinese Population in the Straits Settlement
(1678-1860)

Malacca		Penang*		Singapore	
Year	Population	Year	Population	Year	Population
1678	850				
1750	2,161	1786	nil		
1766	1,390	1812	7,558	1819	nil
1812	1,006	1842	13,822	1830	6,555
1842	6,882	1850	24,188	1850	27,988
1860	10,039	1860	36,222	1860	50,043

Source: Victor Purcell, *The Chinese in Malaya*, pages x-xi
* Penang includes Province Wellesley

Even in the kingdoms and sultanates where the Europeans did not or had not yet established sovereignty (Siam and the Malay states), the Chinese were not a significant presence.

At the close of the seventeenth century, only about 3,000 Chinese were estimated to be living at Ayuthia, then the capital of Siam (present-day Thailand). It was only at the start of the nineteenth century that travellers to Thailand began to comment on their presence.[16]

Victor Purcell, in his book, *The Chinese in Malaya*, stated that the number of Chinese in the Malay states of Perak, Selangor, Negri Simbilan, Pahang, Johore, Kedah, Kelantan, Trengganu and Perlis (present-day Peninsular Malaysia excluding Penang and Malacca) was small until these states came under British protection. In 1839, a British visitor to Johore estimated the local population at 35,000 without mentioning any Chinese presence. As late as 1888, the Chinese population in Pahang was estimated at a few hundred out of a total population of 50,000. For the Malay states as a whole, Purcell accepts the estimate of the total Chinese population at 15-20,000 in 1830.[17]

In the British Borneo states of Sarawak, North Borneo (present-day Sabah) and Brunei, the number of Chinese is even smaller. When Sir James Brooke became the first White Raja of Sarawak in 1841, he sought to bring the Chinese into his sultanate, convinced as he was of their value as industrious workers. Despite such encouragement, the Census of 1871 listed only 4,947 Chinese out of a total population of 128,679. The Chinese population of Brunei in 1889 was much less, estimated at eighty out of an estimated total population of 12-15,000. North Borneo was actually part of the sultanate of Brunei until 1881 when the British government granted a charter to a private company, the British North Borneo Company. The company in trying to develop and people the area, also followed the example of Brooke of Sarawak in bringing in Chinese laborers. By 1883, these totaled about 3,000.[18]

In summary then, the Chinese population of traders and merchants in the ASEAN region totaled around 100,000 prior to the large-scale immigration of Chinese laborers and peasants.

B. *The Dragon's Seed: The Laborers*

Ironically, the large scale immigration of Chinese laborers was initiated by the two ASEAN states which were then *not* under any of the colonial powers — Siam and the Malay states.

In his book, *Double Identity: The Chinese in Modern Thailand*, Richard Coughlin notes that the Chinese were initially a source of cheap and skilled labor in Thailand:

> Bangkok was established as the national capital only at the end of the 18th century after the complete destruction of Ayuthia, the ancient capital, by Burmese armies. From a small river town, Bangkok has grown during the last century into one of the largest cities of the Far East with over a million residents today. For this expansion of the city, the construction of public and private buildings, streets, canals and port facilities, the Chinese furnished the bulk of the skilled and labor semi-skilled labor, and the steady demand for their services during the past 75 years particularly has been a major attraction for immigrant Chinese.[19]

The effect of such large-scale importation of Chinese skilled labor was a significant increase in the size of the Chinese population. By the 1820's, estimates of the size of the Chinese population ranged from 100,000 to 500,000 with 230,000 being the more realistic figure. Moreover, about fifty per cent of the Chinese population was estimated to be concentrated in the Bangkok area.[20]

While not on as large a scale as Siam, the Malay states also brought in Chinese laborers to work the tin mines. As the influx of Chinese laborers grew relative to the small population in the Malay states, 20,000 Chinese out of an estimated total population of 200,000 in 1830, competing Chinese groups started allying themselves with warring Malay sultans. The resulting wars brought in the British from the neighboring Straits Settlement of Malacca, Penang and Singapore. The sultanates of Perak and Selangor came under British protection in 1874 — Negri Simbilan in 1875; Pahang in 1888, Kelantan, Trengganu, Kedah and Perlis in 1909; and Johore in 1914.

In nearby pre-British Borneo, the British came into the picture primarily to settle bitter succession disputes, to rid the area of pirates and more importantly to expand the British empire. The sultan of Brunei, who maintained sovereignty over the territories of Sarawak and North Borneo, was forced to cede them to British control. Sovereignty over Sarawak was obtained with the appointment of Sir James Brooke as the Raja of Sarawak in 1841. The territory of North

Borneo was charted to the British North Borneo Company in 1881. The sultanate of Brunei itself became a British protectorate in 1888.[21]

While Great Britain was busy annexing the Malay and Borneo sultanates into its vast empire, great changes were taking place. The nineteenth century was the age of Europe's industrialization. One of the implications of this radical economic development was the perceived need for a different type of colony. Colonies were no longer to be considered as mere trading outposts or part of a far flung network of naval bases. Colonies under the industrial revolution were transformed into suppliers for the vast amount of raw materials (rubber, tin, tobacco, coffee, sugar, etc.) needed by the industrializing countries of Europe and into markets for the processed goods derived from these raw materials. Furthermore, the invention of the steamship and the opening of the Suez Canal in 1869 rendered such an economic system highly profitable despite the distance of the Southeast Asian colonies from the mother countries in Europe.[22]

A major bottleneck for the continued expansion of the economic system was the lack of cheap labor.[23] Since the European and the American countries had by this time outlawed African slavery, China became the source of cheap labor. Thus developed the so-called coolie labor.[24]

Chinese laborers were brought to their destinations through a process of collection and distribution. First the laborers were gathered at several embarkation points in China: Canton, Swatow, Haik'ou, Amoy. From there, they either went direct to the country and work destination such as Thailand, Indonesia, the Philippines or were sent to a way station such as Hong Kong, Singapore and Penang. From Singapore or Penang, Chinese laborers were either off-loaded or transshipped to the other British colonies (the Malay states primarily but also including South Africa, Australia and New Zealand), to the Dutch East Indies (present-day Indonesia), to Siam through the Northern Malay states and to the Borneo sultanates.[25]

An indication of the magnitude of the traffic in Chinese coolie labor may be found in Table II-2.

Since the Chinese population in the Straits Settlements increased by only 485,219 during the same period (173,861 in 1881 and 659,080 in 1931), we can validly assume that a substantial number went to the Malay states, to Thailand, the Dutch East Indies (Indonesia) and the Borneo sultanates.[26]

In the Malay states (which did not include Singapore, Penang and Malacca), the Chinese population rose from around 100,000 in 1881 to 1,042,397 in 1931. As a consequence of the influx of the Chinese into the Straits Settlements and into the Malay states, the Chinese in fact outnumbered the Malays in British Malaya by 1941. Table II-3 presents the shift in the racial composition of British Malaya.

Table II-2
Chinese Emigrants To and From the Straits Settlements*

Period	Arrivals	Departures	Surplus
1881–1890	1,274,608	110,204	1,164,404
1891–1910	3,227,381	548,389	2,778,992
1911–1920	1,599,338	644,470	954,868
1921–1930	2,417,941	1,172,375	1,245,566
Total	8,619,268	2,475,438	6,143,830

Sources: 1881–1910 figures derived from Ta Chen, *Chinese migrations, with special reference to labor conditions*, page 84. 1911-1930 figures cited by Victor Purcell, *The Chinese in Malaya*, page 205.
* Straits Settlements consist of Singapore, Penang and Malacca. Bulk of migration however, was through Singapore.

Table II-3
Population Ratios in British Malaya*

Year	Malay Population	Chinese Population	Ratio of Malay to Chinese
1911	1,414,197	835,883	1.69
1921	1,627,108	1,173,354	1.39
1931	1,934,900	1,705,915	1.13
1941	2,277,352	2,377,990	0.96

Source: Victor Purcell, *The Chinese in Malaya*, in Map at end of text.
* British Malaya consists of the Malay states and the Straits Settlements.

In 1930, the British enforced the Immigration Restriction Ordinance in British Malaya, thus ending free migration of all races into Malaya. While Chinese laborers were still accepted into the country, strict quotas on residency were imposed. The result was a decline in the influx of Chinese laborers and a sharp reduction in permanent migration. In the period 1936-1940, 914,177 Chinese laborers arrived in British Malaya while 822,604 departed for a small surplus of 91,573.[27]

British Borneo also received its share of the Chinese immigrants. However in terms of absolute number and relative to the native population, the Chinese were not as many or dominant as in British Malaya. In Sarawak, for example, the number of Chinese rose from 4,947 (3.8 per cent of the total population) in 1871 to 123,626 in 1939 to 229,154 (30.8 per cent of the total population) in 1960. In British North Borneo, the number of Chinese increased from 3,000 in 1883 to 50,056 in 1931 to 104,542 (23.0 per cent of the total population) in 1960. In Brunei, the number of Chinese increased from 80 in 1889 to 21,745 (25.9 per cent of the total population) in 1960.[28]

While spared colonization by the European powers, Thailand nevertheless was integrated into the Western economic system.

Under the treaty of friendship and commerce concluded with Great Britain in 1855 as well as under the subsequent treaties with the other Western powers, Thailand was opened to the world market, stimulating increased agricultural and mining production for export. The resulting demand for cheap Chinese labor stimulated an influx of migration and a resulting increase in the Chinese population of Thailand.[29]

In his book, *Chinese Society in Thailand: An Analytical History*, G. William Skinner made a detailed analysis of the influx of Chinese immigrants and the resulting increase in the Chinese population. Table II-4 presents the record of Chinese migration into Thailand from 1882 to 1955. Table II-5 presents the percentage of the Chinese population in relation to the total population of Thailand from 1825 to 1955.

Table II-4
Chinese Migration into Thailand
(000)

Period	Arrivals	Departures	Permanent Migration
1882-1892	177.5	99.4	78.1
1893-1905	455.1	261.9	193.2
1906-1917	815.7	635.5	180.2
1918-1931	1,327.6	827.9	499.7
1932-1945	473.7	381.3	92.4
1946-1955	267.8	107.8	160.0
Total	3,517.4	2,313.8	1,203.6

Source: G. William Skinner, *Chinese Society in Thailand: An Analytical History*, pages 61 and 173.

Table II-5
Chinese Population in Thailand
(1825-1955)
(000)

Year	Chinese Population	Total Population	Percentage of Chinese to Total Population
1825	230	4,750	4.8 %
1850	300	5,20	5.8
1870	383	5,775	6.6
1890	497	6,670	7.5
1910	792	8,305	9.5
1917	906	9,232	9.8
1927	1,333	11,419	11.7
1937	1,734	14,721	11.8
1947	2,124	17,643	2.0
1955	2,315	20,480	1.3

Source: G. William Skinner, *Chinese Society in Thailand: An Analytical History*, pages 79 and 183.

The percentage of Chinese population in relation to the total population reached its peak of 12 per cent in 1947. Thereafter, the percentage steadily declined to 10 per cent in 1970[30] and to eight and a half percent in 1974.[31]

In Indonesia, the Dutch, faced with the same labor shortage problem, reversed their migration policy on the Chinese.[32] The net result of such a reversal of policy was the increase in the Chinese population in absolute numbers and as a percentage of the total population of Java and Madura beginning in 1900. Prior to this date, the trend was a decline in the percentage of the Chinese population to the total population (Table II-6).

Moreover, the bulk of the later migration was to the less populous islands of Sumatra and Dutch West Borneo. Table II-7 shows this shift of the distribution of the Chinese population in Indonesia while Table II-8 shows the effect on the population of Indonesia as a whole.

Table II-6
Chinese Population in Java and Madura
(1860-1961)
(000)

Year	Chinese Population	Total Population	Percentage of Chinese to Total Population
1860	149	12,514	1.19 %
1870	175	16,233	1.08
1880	207	19,541	1.06
1890	242	23,609	1.02
1900	277	28,386	0.98
1905	295	29,979	0.98
1920	384	34,429	1.12
1930	582	40,981	1.42
1956	1,145	59,498*	1.92
1961	1,230	63,059	1.95

Sources: Victor Purcell, *The Chinese in Southeast Asia*, page 380; J. S. Furnivall, *Netherlands India: a Study of Plural Economy*, pages 347 and 408; and Ruth McVey, *Indonesia*, pages 14-15.
* 1956 total population figure estimated from 1930 and 1961 figures.

In the Philippines, the transition to an export commodity economy prompted a shift in the Spanish policy of restricting the number of Chinese residents in the Philippines. In 1850, the Spanish government in the Philippines decreed preferred tax status for Chinese agricultural laborers especially for those who settled in the Visayas. While the change in policy stimulated some migration of Chinese laborers, the influx was not large.[33]

In 1898, when the Philippines became a colony of the United States, the Chinese exclusion laws which were passed primarily to prevent the migration of Chinese laborers to California were also adopted by the American military government in the Philippines. In

Table II-7
Geographic Distribution of the Chinese Population in Indonesia
(1860-1961)
(000)

Year	Java Number	%	Sumatra Number	%	West Borneo Number	%	Others Number	%	Total
1860	150	67.6%	–	–	–	–	72	32.4%	222
1880	207	60.2	94	27.3%	28	8.1%	15	4.4	344
1895	256	54.6	159	33.9	38	8.1	17	3.6	469
1905	295	52.4	195	34.6	48	8.5	25	4.4	563
1920	384	47.5	304	37.6	68	8.4	54	6.7	809
1930	582	47.2	449	36.4	108	8.8	94	7.6	1,233
1956	1,145	52.0	605	27.5	271	12.3	179	8.1	2,200
1961	1,230	50.2	690	28.2	315	12.9	215	8.8	2,450

Source: G. William Skinner, "The Chinese Minority," in Ruth McVey, *Indonesia*, page 100.

Table II-8
Chinese Population in Indonesia
(1825-1955)
(000)

Year	Chinese Population	Total Population	Percentage of Chinese to Total Population
1905	563	37,717	1.49 %
1920	809	49,350	1.64
1930	1,233	60,728	2.03
1956	2,200	91,211*	2.41
1961	2,450	97,085	2.52
1974	3,250	129,120	2.52

Sources: Victor Purcell, *The Chinese in Southeast Asia*, page 386; J. S. Furnivall, *Netherlands India: a Study of Plural Economy*, pages 347 and 408; Ruth McVey, *Indonesia*, pages 14-15; and Yuan-li Wu and Chun-hsi Wu, *Economic Development in Southeast Asia: The Chinese Dimension*, page 133.
* 1956 total population figure estimated from 1930 and 1961 figures.

Table II-9
Chinese Population in the Philippines
(Spanish Period)

Year	Chinese Population	Total Population (000)	Percentage of Chinese to Total Population
1847	5,700	3,815	0.15 %
1864	18,000	4,500	0.40
1886	66,000	5,985	1.10

Source: Victor Purcell, *The Chinese in Southeast Asia*, page 503.

1902, the United States Congress passed the necessary legislation to formally include the Philippines under the Chinese exclusion laws.[34] Table II-9 presents the history of Chinese population in the Philippines during the Spanish period while Table II-10 presents the history of the Chinese population during the American period.

Table II-10
Chinese Population in the Philippines
(American Period)

Year	Chinese Population	Total Population (000)	Percentage of Chinese to Total Population
1903	41,035*	6,988	0.59 %
1918	43,802	10,314	0.42
1939	117,487	16,000	0.73
1947	100,971	19,511	0.52

Source: Victor Purcell, *The Chinese in Southeast Asia*, pages 503-504.
* The drop from the Spanish figures can be explained by the Americans excluding Chinese with Filipino citizenship from the figures, a practice the Philippine government followed.

It is interesting to note that whereas the American government officially excluded the Chinese and the Spanish government officially encouraged their entry, the number of Chinese in the Philippines actually increased substantially during the American period. Purcell attributed such perverse results to the more tolerant implementation of the immigration laws. Thus while the 1960 Census reported a total of 181,626 Chinese residents (non-Filipino citizens) in the Philippines[35], the estimate of the Ethnic or Overseas Chinese (Filipino and non-Filipino citizens) ranged from 500,000 to 900,000. The estimate cited by Yuan-li Wu and Chun-hsi Wu for 1974 was 600,000.

C. The Dragon's Seed: A Profile

While the number of Chinese migrating to Southeast Asia was substantial, the number must be placed in the context of China's population. In 1922, at the height of the Chinese migration, the estimated 5.6 million Overseas Chinese in the world constituted only one and a half percent of the Chinese population.[36] As will be evident in this section, the fact that there were Chinese immigrants was due more to economic imperatives than to social impulses.

The barriers to migration were numerous. For one, the Chinese government was opposed to migration and treated migrants, who belonged to the peasant class anyway, as lawbreakers hardly deserving of protection by their government in their sojourn to the Nanyang countries. For another, the Chinese frown upon desertion of ancestral homes (thus requiring the fiction of "returning home" even among third generation Overseas Chinese). Lastly the trip to the destination aboard coolie ships (considered by many as harsh as the African slave ships) and the hard working conditions were acceptable only if the alternatives were famine and death.[37]

Ta Chen in his books, *Chinese migrations, with special reference to labor* and *Relations of Southeast Asian Chinese with Fukien and Kwan-*

tung Communities, provided ample proof of such motivation. Ta Chen cited statistics on population density, famines, droughts and wars among the provinces of China where migration was most prevalent. Ta Chen also cited surveys conducted in 1934 in which seventy per cent of the respondents cited economic pressure as the principal reason for migrating.[38]

Table II-11 presents population statistics on China during the great migration period. The table highlights two important facts about the Chinese population. First is the drastic drop in population from 390 million in 1842 to 306 million in 1885, indicating the magnitude of the turmoil and devastation that China was going through in this period. Second is that while the Overseas Chinese constituted only one-and-a-half percent of China's population in 1922, the primary sources of these Overseas Chinese were only the two provinces of Fukien and Kwantung (with a 1920 population of 50 million). Four other provinces, Chihli, Hunan, Kiangsi and Kwangsi (with a 1920 population of 100 million) were secondary sources.

Table II-11
Estimated Population of China
(1812-1920)
(000)

Province	1812	1842	1885	1910	1920
Primary Sources					
Fukien	14,779	25,800	23,503	13,100	13,158
Kwantung	19,174	21,153	29,740	27,700	37,168
Sub-total	33,953	46,953	53,243	40,800	50,326
Secondary Sources					
Chihli	27,991	36,880	17,937	32,571	34,187
Hunan	18,653	20,049	21,005	23,600	28,443
Kiangsi	23,047	26,514	24,541	14,500	24,467
Kwangsi	7,314	8,121	5,151	6,500	12,258
Sub-total	77,005	91,564	68,634	77,171	99,355
Other Provinces	228,087	252,250	184,674	190,217	225,656
Grand Total	339,045	390,767	306,551	308,188	375,377

Source: Ta Chen, *Chinese migrations, with special reference to laborr conditions*, page 5.

In summary then, we come to the following conclusions:
1. By the beginning of the nineteenth century (1800 A.D.), the Chinese population in the ASEAN countries consisted mostly of merchants and traders and numbered around 100,000.
2. By the middle of the nineteenth century (1850's), the traders, augmented by migrant artisans, laborers and peasants numbered around 600,000 and were distributed as follows

British Borneo (1880's)	8,000
British Malaya (1860's)	130,000
Dutch East Indies (1860's)	222,000
Philippines (1850's)	10,000
Siam (1860's)	230,000
Total	600,000

3. The mass importation of Chinese labor increased the Chinese population in the ASEAN countries to around four and a half million by the 1930's when such importation was stopped by the British. The Overseas Chinese population became as follows:

British Borneo (1930's)	180,000
British Malaya (1931)	1,700,000
Dutch East Indies (1930)	1,230,000
Philippines (1933)	70,000
Siam (1927)	1,330,000
Total	4,510,000

Figure II-1 presents our conclusion in graphical form.

It may of course be argued that the present-day Overseas Chinese businessmen were drawn primarily from the first and earlier group of Chinese immigrants (the traders) rather than from the second and later group (the laborers). Existing evidence, however favors the opposite view.

In a paper entitled "The Chinese Minority (in Indonesia)" G. William Skinner noted the existence of two distinct groups of Overseas Chinese in Indonesia. The first group known as the *Peranakan Tionghoa* (Chinese children of the Indies) arrived in Indonesia from the eighteenth to the early twentieth century. Beginning the first decade of the century, the second group of Chinese immigrants, known in Indonesian as *Totok* , arrived. If the hypothesis that the economic performance of the Overseas Chinese was due to their traditional role as traders, then we would expect the occupational preference for business of the *Peranakans* to be greater than that of the *Totoks*. G. William Skinner discovered otherwise:

> In regard to livelihood, *Totoks* strongly prefer self-employment and are overwhelmingly found in entrepreneurial occupations. *Peranakans*, more diversified in their occupational distribution, show a preference for the professions and for clerical and staff positions in large enterprises. A 1957 questionnaire study in a West Java town showed that among gainfully employed Chinese family heads, shopowners accounted for 80.5 per cent of the foreign-born *Totoks*, for 57.1 per cent of those Chinese citizens who were born in Indonesia, and for only 44.6 per cent of the *Peranakans* holding Indonesian citizenship. In the case of white-collar positions in large business enterprises, however, the corresponding proportions were 2.2, 6.1 and 15.4 per

FIGURE II-I
EVOLUTION OF OVERSEAS CHINESE ECONOMIC ACTIVITIES IN ASEAN

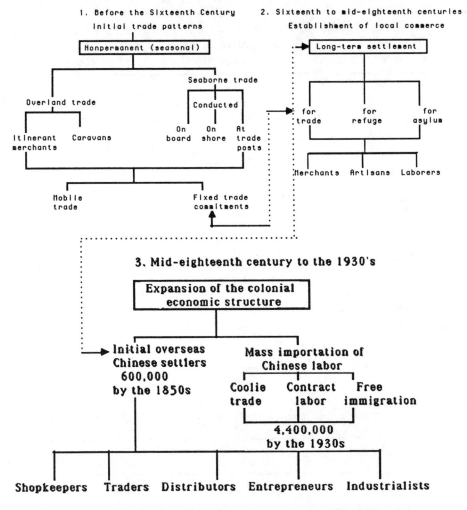

cent. These occupational preferences reflect a marked difference in value orientation. *Totoks* more than *Peranakans* value wealth, frugality, work, self-reliance, and "nerve". *Peranakans* more than *Totoks* value the enjoyment of life, leisure, social standing, and security. A 1957 questionnaire study which I administered in Djakarta showed that in terms of career and success orientation *Totoks* were far ahead of indigeneous Indonesians, and that in this regard *Peranakans* were considerably closer to the Indonesians rather than to the *Totok* Chinese.[39]

D. The Army of Merchants

Whatever differences may exist among the different groups of Overseas Chinese in their occupational preferences, such differences are minor when one compares the occupational preferences of the Overseas Chinese as a whole with those of the indigeneous population. Table II-12 presents such a contrast in terms of the preferred sector of the economy of the Overseas Chinese in five ASEAN countries. Table II-13 presents the occupational distribution of the Overseas Chinese in four ASEAN countries.

Table II-12
Distribution of Overall Labor Force and Chinese Employment
(Per Cent)

Country	Primary	Secondary	Tertiary	Total
Indonesia				
Overall (1971)	60.5	22.2	17.2	100.0
Chinese (1940)	30.8	20.0	49.2	100.0
Malaysia				
Overall (1975)	59.2	15.2	25.6	100.0
Chinese (1975)	26.4	32.1	41.5	100.0
Philippines				
Overall (1972)	54.2	11.1	34.6	100.0
Chinese (1957)	–	11.5	88.5	100.0
Singapore				
Overall (1975)	0.5	35.1	64.4	100.0
Chinese (1973)	0.4	45.3	54.2	100.0
Thailand				
Overall (1969)	78.1	4.6	17.3	100.0
Chinese (1957)	8.0	22.0	70.0	100.0

Source: Yuan-li Wu and Chun-hsi Wu, *Economic Development in Southeast Asia: The Chinese Dimension*, page 38.

Table II-13
Occupational Distribution of Ethnic Chinese in ASEAN Region
(Per Cent)

Occupation	Indonesia (no date)	Malaysia (1970)	Philippines (1954)	Thailand (1955)
Government	0.6	–	–	0.02
Professions	1.5	–	40.0	1.59
Commerce and finance	36.6	24.0	41.0	50.84
Industry and handicraft	20.0	24.0	11.0	19.41
Domestic & other service	2.7	5.0	–	9.75
Agriculture	30.9	29.0	–	1.19
Unskilled	7.7	18.0	8.0	17.21

Source: Yuan-li Wu and Chun-hsi Wu, *Economic Development in Southeast Asia: The Chinese Dimension*, page 137.

The only comparable data on the occupational distribution of the overall population is on Thailand. Table II-14 presents the occupational distribution of the Overseas Chinese compared to the indigneous Thai.

Table II-15 presents the contrast in the geographical distribution of the Overseas Chinese as compared to the indigeneous Thai in the Greater Bangkok area where 50 per cent of the Overseas Chinese in Thailand reside.

Table II-14
Ethnic Occupational Specialization
(Krungthep, Thailand)
(1952)

Occupation	Ethnic Chinese	Ethnic Thai
Government	0.02%	26.87%
Professions	1.59	5.39
Commerce and finance	50.84	25.41
Industry and artisan	19.41	6.08
Domestic and service	9.75	15.11
Agriculture*	1.19	4.13
Unskilled labor	17.21	17.00
Total	100.01%	99.99%

Source: G. William Skinner, *Chinese Society in Thailand: An Analytical History*, page 303.
*The low share of agriculture is explained by the fact that Krungthep is an urban and administrative center. About 80% of the population of Thailand is in agriculture.

Table II-15
Distribution of Greater Bangkok Population
(August 1954)

Area	Ethinic Chinese		Others		Total	
	Number	%	Number	%	Number	%
Central Business Area	265,441	78.1	74,626	21.9	340,067	28.2
Surrounding Area	218,875	44.5	272,456	55.5	491,331	40.7
Outlying Area	67,480	17.9	308,879	82.1	76,359	31.1
Total	551,796	45.7	655,961	54.3	1,207,757	100.0

Source:G. William Skinner, *Chinese Society in Thailand: An Analytical History*, page 206.

E. *The ASEAN Response*

The response of the ASEAN countries, with the exception of Brunei and Singapore, to the perceived dominance of their economy by the Overseas Chinese eventually evolved into the active involvement of the government in the nation's economy.

The initial step was to cut off the flow of immigrants from China, with Indonesia under Sukarno even seeking to reverse the flow back to China or Taiwan. The objectives of such a policy were twofold: to reduce the percentage of the Overseas Chinese population with respect to the total population, and to encourage the process of assimilation by forcing the Overseas Chinese population to choose between retaining their Chinese citizenship (hence returning to China, Taiwan or Hong Kong) or accepting local citizenship (hence integration into the local community).

While the policy showed initial promise, the political climate demanded more immediate results. As a consequence, the ASEAN governments adopted public policies which in effect worked against the objective of assimilation and also increased government intervention in the economy.[40]

The first of such public policies could be termed *exclusion policies*. They officially declared specific industries or economic activities off-limits to the Overseas Chinese. For example, in June of 1942, the government of Thailand declared that twenty-seven industries and occupations were reserved for the employment of Thai citizens only.

The second type of policies could be termed *preference policies*. The government as a matter of policy gave priority to indigenous businessmen. For example, the 1950 *Benteng* program of the Indonesian government gave favorable allocation of foreign exchange to indigenous Indonesian businessmen.

The third type of policies could be termed *support policies*. The government not only gave preference to but actively supported the indigenous businessmen. For example, in 1956 the Philippine government organized the National Marketing Corporation (NAMARCO) to supply Filipino-owned retail stores at subsidized prices.

The fourth type of policies could be termed *indigenization policies*. Under these policies, Overseas Chinese businessmen were required to transfer equity in their businesses to local investors. For example, in 1957 the Indonesian government ordered the indigenization of fifteen industries. Under this order, 50 per cent of the equity of firms in the designated industry had to be transferred to indigenous Indonesians over a period of five years. At the end of this grace period, the remaining 50 per cent would also be sold to indigenous buyers. Such sales were to be paid in installments over a ten-year period. If necessary, even the initial 50 per cent was to be paid gradually out of the anticipated profits of the new indigenous owners.

G. *The Persistent Presence: The Malaysian Case*

The harshness of the policies of the ASEAN governments could be attributed to the continued presence in the economy of the Overseas Chinese despite the previous government policies. Among the ASEAN countries, the government of Malaysia has adopted the most comprehensive public policies.

In 1971, the government of Malaysia formally adopted the New

Economic Policy (NEP).[41] The NEP sought to restructure Malaysian society so as to achieve by 1990 a community where all the racial groups consisting of the Malays (*Bumiputras*), the Chinese and the Indians will participate as full partners in the socio-economic development of the nation. The NEP outlined a two-pronged approach to the attainment of such an objective: *Poverty Eradication and Income Equalization*[42]

The NEP objective of poverty eradication called for a pattern of development which would permit increased participation and involvement of the poor in the economic prosperity of the nation. This increased participation and involvement was to be achieved through land development, increase in agricultural productivity especially through irrigation projects, and the absorption of the rapidly growing labor force into higher income jobs in the industrial and services sector.

Specific programs were undertaken to help specific target groups; i.e. rubber smallholders, padi (rice) farmers, coconut smallholders, estate workers, fishermen. The urban poor were also benefitted by the provision of public facilities, low-cost housing projects and even assistance to petty traders in the acquisition of stalls.

Prior to the NEP, the Malaysian government had sought to develop *bumiputra* entrepreneurs through such government organizations as the *Majlis Amanah Rakyat* (MARA) and the Urban Development Authority (UDA). The NEP, however spawned a more aggressive government corporation called *Perbandaan Nasional* (PERNAS). PERNAS pursued an initial strategy of being the corporate entrepreneur for the *Bumiputra* sector and the designated *Bumiputra* partner for foreign investors in Malaysia. Eventually, the strategy was expanded to buy out the British companies in Malaysia. The success of PERNAS in taking over SIME DARBY, the biggest company in Southeast Asia stimulated the creation of *Permodalan Nasional* (PNB). In addition to assuming the function of acquiring the remaining British companies in Malaysia, PNB embarked on a program of transferring the shares in such acquired companies to *Bumiputra* investors.

Despite the considerable progress that was achieved in eradicating povery and in raising the income of the Malay, the gap between the Chinese and the Malays persisted. Table II-16 presents the evidence for such a gap.

H.*Historical Analysis*

Given the history of the Overseas Chinese in ASEAN countries as the foundation, I now proceed to the use of historical analysis to identify the independent variables that have influenced our dependent variable: the economic success of the Overseas Chinese in ASEAN. Several propositions may be considered:

Table II-16
Racial Mean Incomes in Peninsular Malaysia
(M $ per household per month)

Year	Chinese	Malay	Chinese/Malay
1957/58	300	139	2.158 x
1967/68	349	163	2.141
1970	399	177	2.254
———————————————— New Economic Policy ————————			
1973	534	242	2.207
1976	787	345	2.281
1979	1,094	513	2.132

Sources: Household Budget Survey - Federation of Malaya 1957-58, SRM/Ford Social and Economic Survey 1967/68, Post Enumeration Survey of the 1970 population census, and *The Fourth Malaysia Plan 1981-1985.*

Proposition # 1: Trader Tradition Hypothesis
The hypothesis that the success of the Overseas Chinese in the ASEAN countries is attributable to their tradition of skills and resources as traders *can not* be accepted.

Unlike the European Jews[43] arriving in nineteenth century America or even the American Multinationals entering the global market in the twentieth century, the Overseas Chinese, drawn from the peasant and labor class, enjoyed neither superior commercial skills nor ample resources in their rise to economic dominance in the ASEAN region.

It could even be argued that Imperial China herself did not possess such skills and resources even in her elite class. The society of Imperial China in the Confucian tradition glorified the scholar as the "superior man," stressed the virtue of agricultural work and belittled the importance of merchants. Thus in the hierarchy of traditional social values, the scholar was at the apex while the merchant was at the bottom, below the farmer and the artisan.[44]

This value system was only challenged at the time that the Chinese laborers were starting their migration to the ASEAN countries. Yen-P'ing Hao, in his book entitled *The Comprador in Nineteenth Century China: Bridge between East and West*, pinpoints as agent of change the comprador who acted as the intermediary or middleman between the foreign merchants and the Chinese society and government:

> The significance of the comprador in the crucial period of China's early industrialization lay not only in his being rich but also in his ability to combine ownership of capital with entrepreneurial skill. Still more important was the fact that, as one of the first Chinese to

experience direct and extensive contact with Westerners, he first saw the profits and promises of modern industry. Such knowledge was invaluable at the time, since it could hardly have been acquired otherwise. It was not that he had become disillusioned with traditional business, but that he had become familiar with the superior advantages of modern enterprises. He accordingly was the first to enter the modern fields of steamship navigation, mining, milling, and finally manufacturing, and thus became a pioneer in China's industrialization effort.[45]

It therefore does not come as a surprise that China's first modern entrepreneur was trained as a comprador of Jardines, a British trading company. Kwang-ching Liu, in his paper entitled, "A Chinese Entrepreneur," tells the story of Tong King-sing, Jardine comprador from 1863 to 1873 and China's first modern entrepreneur:

> Tong King-sing is all but forgotten by British businessmen today, but he was perhaps the most notable personage with a comprador background in modern Chinese history. He was China's first modern entrepreneur - modern in the sense that he dealt with such products of the Industrial Revolution as steamships, steam-driven mining equipment and the railway, and in the sense that he succeeded in organizing commercial capital into joint-stock companies that issued shares to the public. He was the moving spirit of the China Merchant's Steam Navigation Company during the first decade of its long history. He was the founder of the Kaiping Mines near Tangshan in North China, which he managed until his death in 1892.[46]

As further evidence that the economic performance of the overseas Chinese *did not*.derive from any commercial skills learned in Imperial China, we note the attempt of the Imperial Chinese government to recruit Overseas Chinese businessmen to assist in the modernization of the Chinese economy. Michael Godley, in his book, *The Mandarin-capitalist from Nanyang: Overseas Chinese enterprise in the modernization of China 1893-1911* provides a history of that attempt:

> The following pages will outline the development, fruits and legacy of an important, if tardy, campaign to modernize pre-1911 China with the capital and skills of the overseas Chinese. Beginning with the discovery of the plight of coolie laborers in the 1860s, the Ch'ing dynasty shaped a policy which, in its final form, granted returning businessmen a major part in economic affairs. Gradually, the strategic emphasis shifted from the protection of workers to the encouragement of renewed contacts with the motherland to the outright exploitation of overseas experience and wealth.[47]

Proposition #2: Chinese Minority Hypothesis
Given that the success of the Overseas Chinese in the ASEAN region *cannot* be attributed to superior skills or greater resources and given the economic performance of the Overseas Chinese despite such lack of superior skills and resources vis-a-vis the local population, we are left with the hypothesis that the success of the Overseas Chinese in the ASEAN *can only* be explained by the two characteristics that distinguished them in the ASEAN countries: the fact that they were a minority group (except for Singapore) and that they were Chinese with Chinese values and social organizations.

Proposition #3: Chinese rather than Minority Group Hypothesis
Further historical analysis would indicate that the success of the Overseas Chinese in the ASEAN is due more to the fact that they were Chinese rather than that they were a minority group.

In addition to the fact that the Chinese of Singapore continued to be successful despite their majority status, the more compelling argument for this hypothesis is the fact that the economic performance of other distinct minority groups was not comparable to that of the Overseas Chinese. For our purposes the contrast in the economic performance between the Indians and the Chinese who both came to Malaysia as mining and agricultural workers is a persuasive argument that what contributed more to the success of the Overseas Chinese was more that they were Chinese than that they were a minority group.[48] Table II-17 shows that while the income of the Indians was higher than that of the Malays, it was not comparable to the income of the Chinese.

Table II-17
Racial Mean Incomes in Peninsular Malaysia
(M $ per household per month)

Year	Chinese	Indian	Chinese/Indian
1957/58	300	237	1.266 x
1967/68	349	260	1.342
1970	399	310	1.287
———————— New Economic Policy ————————			
1973	534	408	1.309
1976	787	538	1.463
1979	1,094	776	1.410

Sources: Household Budget Survey – Federation of Malaya 1957-58, SRM/Ford Social and Economic Survey 1967/68, Post Enumeration Survey of the 1970 population census, and *The Fourth Malaysia Plan 1981-1985.*

The Indian minority group provides an interesting control group with respect to the Chinese minority.[49] For one, Indian minority groups in East Africa[50] and Burma demonstrated entrepreneurial success when they came in as traders and businessmen rather than as laborers. Burma provides a case study of the entry of such type of Indian minority group.

When Great Britain, at the height of her imperial power completed the annexation of Burma in 1886, she did not distinguish the Burmans from the Indians. As a consequence, Burma became an integral part of British India and the system of laws, regulation and administration which prevailed in British India were also imposed on Burma. Economically the most adverse consequence was to open up the economy of Burma to Indian businessmen, called *chettyars*, at a time of great economic activity. The opening of the Suez Canal, the discovery of oil, and the cultivation of the rich agricultural plains of Irrawaddy transformed Burma into an oil-producing and rice-exporting country. Unfortunately, the main beneficiaries of this economic boom were the non-Burman. Among the non-Burman beneficiaries were the Indian *chettyars*. At the end of British rule in the 1940's, two-thirds of all rice lands were held by non-resident landlords who were mainly *chettyars*.[51] Interestingly, when the Burmese attained independence and implemented a radical land reform program (rendered politically easy, given the alien status of the *chettyars*), their place as the premier business group was taken over by the Chinese.[52]

Preposition #4 : The ASEAN environment is a qualifying condition for Overseas Chinese economic success
While the Overseas Chinese have been successful economically in the ASEAN countries and even in the other Southeast Asian countries of Burma, Cambodia, Laos and Vietnam their economic successes *have not been repeated* either in the developed economy of the United States or in developing the economy of China itself.

In their attempt to assist their mother country, China, to attain economic development during the 1910's, the Overseas Chinese have not been successful.[53] More importantly, Chinese immigrants in the United States have not shown a preference for entrepeneurship on as widespread a level as their counterparts in the ASEAN region. In his book, *The Economics and Politics of Race: An International Perspective*, Thomas Sowell notes that "Unlike southeast Asia, the United States already had entrepreneurs, investors, retailers, bankers, and other important economic roles filled by the

Chinese in the far east." Moreover, Sowell presents statistics which show that the Chinese in the United States have chosen to move into professional fields and have achieved a different type of economic success.

In 1920, more than one-fourth of all Chinese men in the United States were laundry workers, ten per cent were restaurant workers and the rest were in semi-skilled work as personal servants, cooks or agricultural workers. Less than one per cent had professional occupations. By 1940, the proportion of Chinese who worked in professional level occupations had risen was less than half that among whites. By 1960, the Chinese proportion had exceeded that of the whites. And by 1970, the proportion of Chinese who worked in professional level occupations had risen to 30 per cent, *double* that of the white population. Correspondingly, the income of the Chinese Americans passed the national average in 1959 and the gap has continued to widen.[54].

In summary then, our historical analysis of the Overseas Chinese leads us to the following general proposition:

General Proposition: The economic success of the Overseas Chinese in the ASEAN region can be attributed to a combination of two major factors:
a)   The Value and Social System of the Overseas Chinese, and
b)   The ASEAN environment

To explain how the combination of the two major factors of the value and social system of the Overseas Chinese and the ASEAN environment has resulted in such an economic performance, we now turn to the Business Policy Hypothesis for our conceptual framework.

NOTES

1. See chapter one stating views of Prime Minister Mahathir bin Mohamad on the reasons for the economic dominance of the Chinese in Malaysia. Views were taken from Mahathir bin Mohamad, *The Malay Dilemma* (Singapore: Times Books International, 1970), p. 32-54.
2. D. Jenkins, "Traders who came to stay," *Far East Economic Review*, September 21, 1979.
3. Victor Purcell, *The Chinese in Southeast Asia* (London: Oxford University Press, 1965), p. 11.
4. Ibid., pp. 13, 19 and 257.
5. Ibid., p. 12.
6. Ibid., pp. 87 and 507.
7. Ibid., pp. 407-411.
8. Ibid., p. xi.
9. David J. Steinberg et al., *In Search of Southeast Asia: A Modern History* (New York: Praeger Publishers, 1971), p. 216.
10. Lennox A. Mills, *Southeast Asia: Illusion and Reality in Politics and Economics* (Minneapolis: University of Minnesota Press, 1964), page 110.

11. Purcell, *The Chinese in Southeast Asia*, pp. 391-392.
12. Ibid., pp. 396-397.
13. Ibid., pp. 405-406.
14. Ibid., pp. 421-425. However, population of Dutch West Borneo derived from G. William Skinner, "The Chinese Minority," in Ruth McVey, *Indonesia* (New Haven: Yale University Press, 1963), p. 100.
15. Purcell, *The Chinese in Southeast Asia*, p. 501-503. However, population estimates of Chinese in the Philippines derived from Edgar Wickberg, *The Chinese in Philippine Life, 1850-1898* (New Haven: Yale University Press, 1965), p. 61. Purcell's figure was 10,000; Wickberg cites the 1847 Census for his estimate while Purcell uses the estimate of a writer during that period.
16. Purcell, *The Chinese in Southeast Asia* p. 83.
17. Purcell, *The Chinese in Malaya* (Kuala Lumpur: Oxford University Press, 1968), p. xi.
18. Purcell, *The Chinese in Southeast Asia*, p. 364-375.
19. R.J. Coughlin, *Double Identity: The Chinese in Modern Thailand* (Hong Kong: Hong Kong University Press, 1960), p. 117.
20. G. William Skinner, *Chinese Society in Thailand: An Analytical History* (Ithaca, New York: Cornell University Press, 1957), p. 69-71.
21. Purcell, *The Chinese in Malaya*, pp. xi-xii.
22. Milton Osborne, *Southeast Asia: An Introductory History* (Sydney: George Allen & Unwin, 1983), p 76-77.
23. Lea E. Williams, *The Future of the Overseas Chinese in Southeast Asia* (New York: McGraw-Hill Book Company, 1966), p. 39.
24. Lois Mitchison, *The Overseas Chinese: A Background Book* (London: The Bodley Head, 1961), p. 17-18.
25. Ta Chen, *Chinese migrations with special reference to labor conditions* (Taipei: Ch'eng-Wen Publishing Company, 1967), p. 13-14.
26. In looking at the same figures, Yuan-li Wu and Chun-hsi Wu reached a similar conclusion. See Yuan-li Wu and Chun-hsi Wu, *Economic Development in Southeast Asia: The Chinese Dimension* (Stanford: Hoover Institution Press, 1980), p. 91.
27. Purcell, *The Chinese in Malaya*, p. 205-206.
28. Purcell, *The Chinese in Southeast Asia*, p. 357-363.
29. Ibid., p. 102.
30. Mary F. Sommers Heidhues, *Southeast Asia's Chinese Minorities* (Melbourne: Longman Australia, 1974), p. 3.
31. Table I-1.
32. The Dutch reversed their policy despite the fact that they had an alternative source of labor. Java even at that time was already densely populated. I would explain their preference for Chinese labor as simply a matter of economics. When the cost of Chinese labor increased in the 1930s, the Dutch switched to the use of Javanese labor. See Victor Purcell, *The Chinese in Southeast Asia* (London: Oxford University Press, 1965), p. 433-434 and p. 463-465.
33. Edgar Wickberg, *The Chinese in Philippine Life, 1850-1898* (New Haven: Yale University Press, 1965), p. 56.
34. Purcell, *The Chinese in Southeast Asia*, p. 535.
35. Ibid., p. 503-504.
36. Ta Chen, *Chinese Migrations with special reference to labor conditions* (Taipei: Ch'eng-Wen Publishing Company, 1967), p. 15. I excluded from his estimate of 8,179,582 the Chinese population of Formosa and Hong Kong which I considered part of China. Figure on total Chinese population taken from page 5.
37. Purcell, *The Chinese in Southeast Asia*, p. 24-30.
38. Ta Chen, *Chinese Migrations with special reference to labor conditions* (Taipei: Ch'eng-Wen Publishing Company, 1967), p. 5-11 and p. 16-17 for the statistics and Ta Chen, *Relations of Southeast Asian Chinese with Fukien and Kwantung Communities* (Ch'angsha: The Commercial Press, 1937), p. 48 for the survey.
39. G. William Skinner, "The Chinese Minority," in Ruth McVey, *Indonesia* (New Haven: Yale University Press, 1963), p. 105-107.

48   The Overseas Chinese in ASEAN

40. For a listing of restrictions on Ethnic-Chinese economic activities, see Yuan-li Wu and Chun-hsi Wu, *Economic Development in Southeast Asia: The Chinese Dimension* (Stanford: Hoover Institution Press. 1980), p. 173-170.
41. More specifically, *The Second Malaysia Plan (SMP) 1971-1975* (Kuala Lumpur: Government Press, 1971).
42. Since the Malaysian Malays had a lower income than the Malaysian Chinese and since the percentage of Malaysian Malays below the official poverty line was greater than that of the Malaysian Chinese, the twin objectives of poverty eradication and income equalization allowed the Malaysian government to pursue a non-discriminatory and very laudable policy while at the same time favoring the Malaysian Malays in reality.
43. The Overseas Chinese in Southeast Asia have, however been consistently termed the "Jews of the East". In 1914, King Rama VI of Thailand, writing under the pen name of "Asavabahu" wrote a series of articles entitled "The Jews of the East" which was highly critical of the Chinese in Thailand. See Kenneth Perry Landon, *The Chinese in Thailand* (London: Oxford University Press), pages 34-42. Alexander Garth in his book, *Silent Invasion: The Chinese in Southeast Asia* (London: MacDonald & Company (Publishers) Limited, 1973), includes a chapter entitled "Jews of the East," p. 45-65. Scholars have been intrigued by the similarity between the Jews and the Chinese. See D. Stanley Eitzen, "Two Minorities: The Jews of Poland and the Chinese of the Philippines," *Jewish Journal of Sociology*, 1960, Volume 10, Number 2, p. 221-240. Historians such as Lennox Mills and economists such as Thomas Sowell have also made similar comparisons.
44. Michael Godley, *The Mandarin-capitalists from Nanyang: Overseas Chinese enterprise in the modernization of China 893-1911* (Cambridge: Cambridge University Press, 1981), p. 32-35.
45. Yen-p'ing Hao, *The Comprador in Nineteenth Century China: Bridge between East and West* (Cambridge, MA: Harvard University Press, 1970), p. 5.
46. Kwang-ching Liu, "A Chinese Entrepreneur", in Maggie Keswick, *The Thistle and the Jade: A Celebration of 150 Years of Jardine Matheson & Company* (London: Octopus Books Ltd., 1982), p. 104.
47. Michael Godley, *The Mandarin-capitalists from Nanyang: Overseas Chinese enterprise in the modernization of China 893-1911* (Cambridge: Cambridge University Press, 1981) p. 3.
48. More specifically, their success is due to the joint intersection of their Chinese culture and their minority status.
49. For a description of the Indian minority in Southeast Asia see Virginia Thompson and Richard Adloff, *Minority Problems in Southeast Asia* (Stanford: Stanford University Press, 1955), p. 59-134.
50. K. Yambert, "Alien Traders and Ruling Elites: The Overseas Chinese in Southeast Asia and the Indians in East Africa," *Ethnic Groups*, January 1, 1981.
51. For the historical background on British Burma, see Kalyani Bandyopadhyaya, *Burma and Indonesia: Comparative Political Economy and Foreign Policy* (New Delhi: South Asian Publishers, 1983), page 5. For report on the extent of dominance of the Burmese Economy by the Indian *Chettyars* see J. Russel Andrus, *Burmese Economic Life* (Stanford: Stanford University Press, 1948), pages 67-71 and Frank N. Trager, *Burma: From Kingdom To Republic: A Historical and Political Analysis* (London: Pall Mall Press, 1966), p. 146.
52. Purcell, *The Chinese in Southeast Asia*, p. 45.
53. Godley, *The Mandarin-capitalists from Nanyang: Overseas Chinese enterprise in the modernization of China 1893-1911*.
54. Thomas Sowell, *The Economics and Politics of Race: An International Perspective* (New York: William Morrow and Company, Inc., 1983), p. 45-49.

CHAPTER III
THE BUSINESS POLICY HYPOTHESIS

A.*Rationale for Exposition on Business Policy Framework*

This book seeks to reach two major audiences; those interested in the economic performance of the Overseas Chinese in the ASEAN region and those interested in the use of the business policy framework in explaining that economic performance. In Chapter II, I provided information on the Overseas Chinese in ASEAN for the business policy audience which is not familar with this business group. In Chapter III, I propose to explain the business policy framework for the Overseas Chinese audience which is not familiar with it.

My objective in this chapter is threefold:
1) to provide a summary of business policy concepts which would allow the non-business policy audience to follow my arguments without being hindered by the jargon, or at the very least to provide a starting point for further study[1];
2) to highlight those specific business policy concepts which I intend to use in explaining the economic performance of the Overseas Chinese;
3) to lay the foundation for linking those business concepts to specific business activities of the Overseas Chinese.

Admittedly, this attempt to link concepts to practices may move the reader to immediately reject the attempt for it is without proof. I therefore remind the reader that in this chapter, I shall merely be stating my hypothesis (i.e. proposed explanation) rather than proving my thesis (i.e. proven explanation).

B. *Business Policy and Business Strategy: The Academic Origins*

In 1911 the Harvard Business School introduced a new course into its curriculum called Business Policy.[2] This course as it eventually evolved was envisioned, in the words of one of the the pioneering professors, Kenneth R. Andrews, as the integrative capstone course in the Master in Business Administration (M.B.A.) curriculum:

> one devoted to the problems of the company *as a whole* as seen from the perspective of the president or chief executive. Its format has traditionally included complex cases, continually renewed, which present as far as practicable the total situation of the company. Students are asked to analyze the state of the company, to identify the principal problems in its situation, and to prescribe a program of action. They soon discover that only the determination of suitable objectives make possible a satisfactorily rational choice among action alternatives. The

discussion of individual companies therefore matures into a consideration of how to formulate an appropriate pattern of purpose and policy and how to convert plans into results.[3]

To provide a theoretical framework for the teaching of business policy, the Harvard Business School faculty developed the concept of Corporate Strategy which Andrews again defined as follows:

> Corporate strategy is the pattern of decisions in a company that determines and reveals its objectives, purposes, or goals, produces the principal policies and plans for achieving these goals, and defines the range of business the company is to pursue, the kind of economic and human organization it is or intends to be, and the nature of the economic and non-economic contribution it intends to make to its shareholders, employees, customers and communities . . . Corporate strategy defines the business in which a company will compete, preferably in a way that focuses resources to convert distinctive competence into competitive advantage.[4]

Elaborating further on the concept of strategy, Andrews identified the four components of corporate strategy: market opportunity, corporate competence and resources, personal values and aspirations, and acknowledged obligation to segments of society other than stockholders. Andrews' thesis was that the combination of these four components was necessary not only in formulating strategy (deciding what to do) but also in implementing strategy as well (achieving results). Figure III-1 presents the Andrews framework.

While acknowledged as a successful pedagogical concept, business or corporate strategy did not initially elicit interest from either management theorists[5] or management practitioners.[6] Several reasons can be given for this neglect. For one, the interest of management theorists and management practitioners lay elsewhere.[7] For another, the concept of corporate strategy was perceived more as a normative rather than a descriptive model (i.e. what is taught in school but what is not followed in practice).

In 1962, Alfred Chandler's *Strategy and Structure: Chapters in the History of American Industrial Enterprise*[8] challenged the prevailing perception and initiated the still-continuing interest of both scholars and practitioners in business policy in general and corporate strategy in particular.

Examining briefly the administrative histories of close to a hundred of America's largest enterprises (fifty with the largest assets in 1909 and seventy with the largest assets in 1948) and more intensely the administrative histories of the four American companies which first created the modern "decentralized" form of organization – du Pont, General Motors, Standard Oil (New Jersey), and

FIGURE III-1
ANDREW'S STRATEGY FRAMEWORK

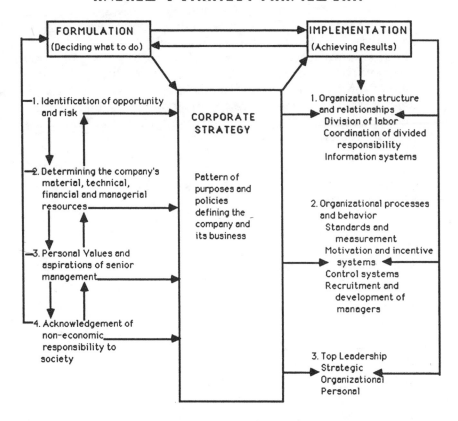

Source: Kenneth R. Andrews, *The Concept of Corporate Strategy, Revised Edition,* page 28.

Sears, Roebuck and Company – Chandler reached the following conclusions:

1. Insofar as the planning and carrying out of a company's growth may be considered strategy, the management of the companies in question has been formulating and implementing strategy.

2. The structure of a company which can be defined as the design of organization through which the enterprise is administered follows strategy. Thus, the structure of a company can not be understood, much less evaluated without prior knowledge and understanding of a company's strategy.[9]

The interest which the book generated among both management theorists and management practitioners resulted in the explosion of research and publications which can be classified as follows:

1. The formulation of different concepts of strategy. For example, Charles Hofer and Dan Schendel, in their book entitled *Strategy*

Formulation: Analytical Concepts, present a table comparing the three concepts of strategy of Chandler, Andrews and Ansoff, add nine other concepts by Cannon, Katz, Ackoff, McNichols, Newman & Logan, Uyeterhoeven, Glueck and Steiner & Miner and present their own, Hofer & Schendel.[10]

2. The attempts to test the value and validity of business policy and strategy concepts. For example, Jay Galbraith and Daniel Nathanson in their book entitled, Strategy Implementation:The Role of Structure and Process,[11] provide a summary of the research that has been undertaken to provide empirical foundations for the business policy concepts.

3. The attempt to link the concepts of the new discipline to the older and more established concepts in other fields of discipline. Examples of such attempts are those of the economist Oliver Williamson in his book, Markets and Hierarchies[12], of the sociologist James Thompson in his book,Organizations in Action[13], and of business professor Bruce Scott, in his papers entitled "Stages of Corporate Development (Part I and Part II)."

4. The attempt to extend the applicability of the concepts developed beyond the field of business. For example, the Harvard Business School has several policy cases on non-profit organizations.

C. Alternative Strategy Frameworks

In the aftermath of the Chandler study, two alternative strategy frameworks initially gained acceptance. Andrews' concepts were formalized initially in a textbook entitled Business Policy: Text and Cases, which he co-authored with Edmund Learned, C. Roland Christensen, and William Guth in 1965.[14] In 1971 his ideas and concepts on corporate strategy were published separately in a book entitled The Concept of Corporate Strategy.[15]

The framework presented by Andrews represented a formalization of the concepts developed by the Harvard Business School faculty in their core course, Business Policy. Igor Ansoff, in his 1965 book entitled Corporate Strategy: An Analytic Approach to Business Policy for Growth and Expansion[16] provided the first alternative approach to strategy formulation approach of the Harvard Business School method.

Ansoff viewed strategy as the common thread among an organization's product/markets and activities that defined the essential nature of the business that the organization was in and planned to be in the future. Ansoff then identified the four components that such a common thread would possess: a product/market scope, a growth vector, competitive advantage, and synergy. Ansoff's unique contributions could be in the use of the matrix

FIGURE III-2
PRODUCT/MISSION MATRIX

Product / Mission	Present	New
Present	Market Penetration	Product Development
New	Market Development	Diversification

Source: Igor Ansoff, *Corporate Strategy: An Analytic Approach to Business Policy for Growth and Expansion*, page 109.

(forever the staple of all future strategy theorists) and the concept of synergy (defined as the 2 + 2 = 5 effect). Figure III-2 presents the initial use of the matrix by Ansoff.

In the ensuing years since the pioneering work of Andrews and Ansoff, several management theorists have sought to present their own concepts of corporate strategy. But the next breakthrough must be attributed to another group of management experts; the management consultants.

In 1979, Bruce D. Henderson, founder and chief executive of the Boston Consulting Group, published in book form the essays he wrote for clients of the company over the previous ten years. In that book, entitled *Henderson on Corporate Strategy*, Henderson presented the strategy concepts which established the reputation of his consulting firm. The most notable of such concepts was what has been termed "The Product Portfolio Mix":

> To be successful, a company should have a portfolio of products with different growth rates and different market shares. The portfolio composition is a function of the balance between cash flows. High growth products require cash inputs to grow. Low growth products should generate excess cash. Both kinds are needed simultaneously ...
>
> The balanced portfolio has "stars" whose high share and high growth assure the future; "cash cows" that supply funds for that

future growth; and "problem children" to be converted into "stars" with the added funds. "Dogs" are not necessary. They are evidence of failure either to obtain a leadership position during the growth phase, or to get out and cut the losses.[17]

Figure III-3 presents the product portfolio mix in matrix form.

FIGURE III-3
PRODUCT PORTFOLIO MIX

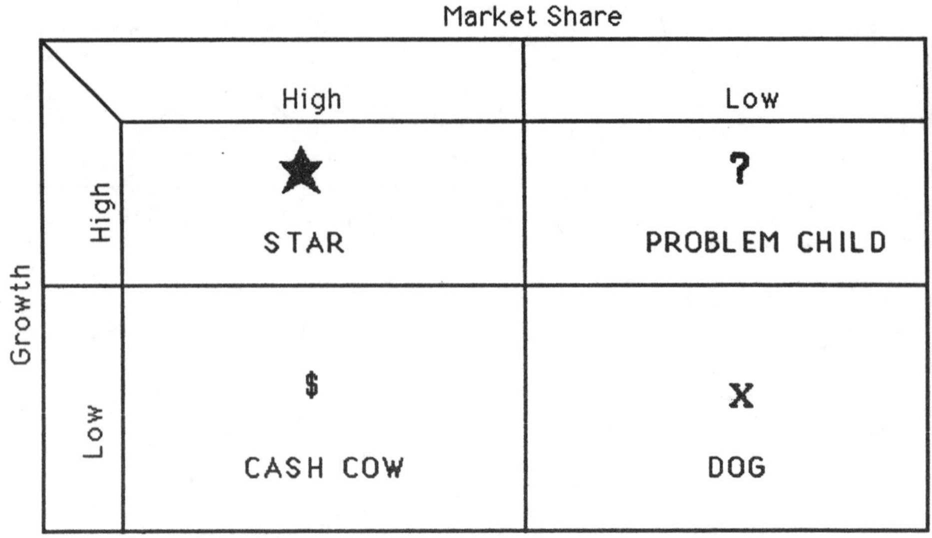

Market Share

	High	Low
High	★ STAR	? PROBLEM CHILD
Low	$ CASH COW	X DOG

Growth

Source: Bruce D. Henderson, Henderson on Corporate Strategy, page 170.

The next conceptual breakthrough in corporate strategy can be found in the books of Michael E. Porter, *Competitive Strategy: Techniques for Analysing Industries and Competitors*, (1980) and *Competitive Advantage: Creating and Sustaining Superior Performance* (1985). Porter, building on what he termed the classical approaches to strategy formulation introduced the concept of generic competitive strategies, the forces driving industry competition, the value chain concept as well as various frameworks for successfully conducting company, industry and competitor analysis.[18]

Figure III-4 presents the forces driving industry competitiveness while Figure III-5 presents the three generic strategies.

FIGURE III-4
THE FIVE COMPETITIVE FORCES
THAT
DETERMINE INDUSTRY PROFITABILITY

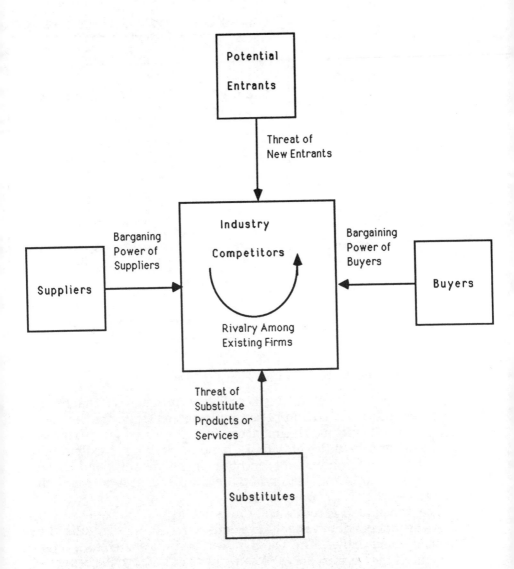

Source: Michael E. Porter, *Competitive Advantage: Creating and Sustaining Superior Performance*, page 5.

FIGURE III-5
GENERIC COMPETITIVE STRATEGIES

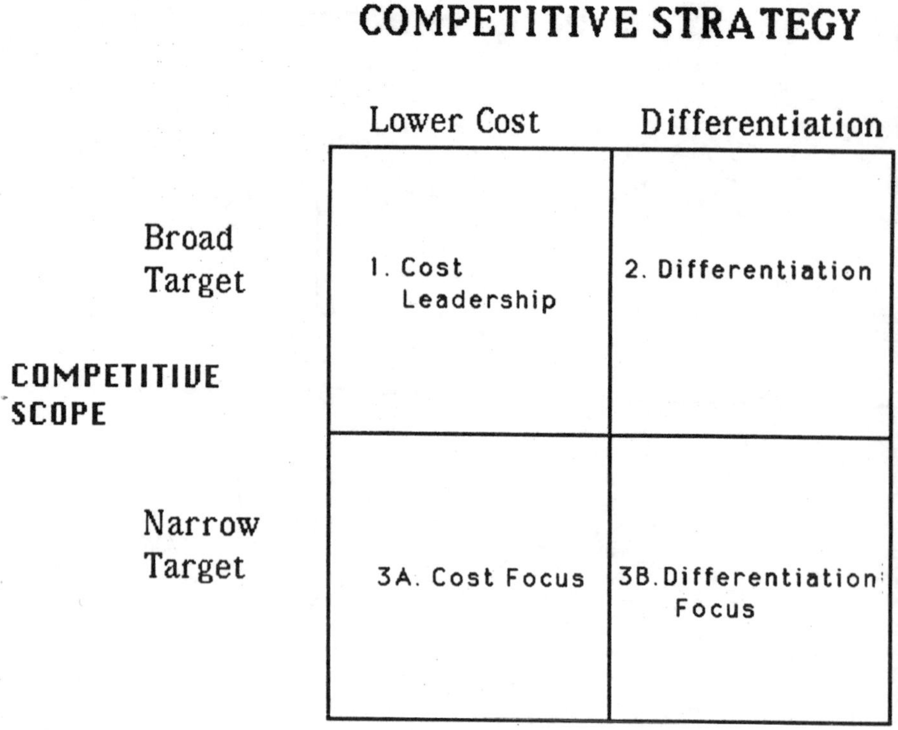

COMPETITIVE STRATEGY

	Lower Cost	Differentiation
Broad Target	1. Cost Leadership	2. Differentiation
Narrow Target	3A. Cost Focus	3B. Differentiation Focus

COMPETITIVE SCOPE

Source: Michael E. Porter, *Competitive Advantage: Creating and Sustaining Superior Performance*, page 12.

D. *The Validity of the Business Policy Hypothesis*

The basic premise of the Business Policy Hypothesis is that firms with better formulated and better implemented strategies perform better than other firms. The initial evidence presented was of course in the historical studies of Alfred Chandler. Seeking to extend the validity of the hypothesis beyond the large companies and to the present environment, researchers encountered several research design issues.

The principal research issue is the tautology that the better strategies (the independent variable) are defined by the better results (the dependent variable). The usual research studies therefore have compared the performances of companies doing formal corporate strategy formulation (or strategic planning) with the performances of similar companies (same size, same industry, etc.) *not* doing formal strategy formulation.

As expected, the results were mixed. Karger and Malik studied the performance over a period of ten years of nineteen planning and nineteen nonplanning firms in the machinery, electronic, and chemical industries. Their findings indicated that formal planners significantly outperformed the nonplanner.[19] Rue and Fulmer came out with opposite conclusions. After surveying the planning practices and the performances of 432 firms in three main industrial groups – durables, nondurables, and services – Rue and Fulmer concluded that in service industries the nonplanners outperformed the planners in all instances but that in durable-goods industries the planners outperformed the nonplanners in all instances.[20]

The proponents of the business policy hypothesis have, of course not depended on the above type of surveys to prove the validity of their hypothesis. They advance more compelling arguments for the validity of the hypothesis they advocate.

1. They point out that the business policy concepts they have advocated are grounded in the older and firmer disciplines of economics and mathematics. They argue, for example that the concept of distinctive competence is based on the economic theory of comparative advantage, that the concept of building on strength is validated by the economic theory of specialization and that concepts of competitive strategy are based on rules postulated by the special branch of mathematical economics called Game Theory.

2. They point to the widespread acceptance of the concept of corporate strategy by a significant number of corporations.

3. They point to the widespread diffusion of the concepts of corporate strategy beyond the field of business to other fields of endeavor such as the public sector and even to other non-profit organizations such as private schools and quasi-public museums. Moreover, Bruce R. Scott, John W. Rosenblum and Audrey T. Sproat of the Harvard Business School extended the applications of the concepts to analysis of countries. In their 1980 book entitled *Case Studies in Political Economy: Japan 1854-1977*, they used the business policy framework to do country analysis:

> To accomplish this analysis, it is useful to regard the nation state as a purposeful entity, in much the same way that many analysts choose to view the firm. In both instances, of course, an extraordinary simplication is involved. Decisions, public and private, are the outcome of complicated processes of bargaining and negotiating and the use of power which we call politics. To posit a rational manager of the processes is certainly not of much descriptive value or perhaps of much normative value. On the other hand , this assumption and the framework of analysis that it facilitates provide a significant aid to

business managers in improving their prediction about the future directions of national economies. The framework offers a useful format for the organization of data and a place to start in analyzing national policy.[21]

Assuming the validity of the business policy hypothesis, two other research issues attracted the attention of business policy researchers: determining *as an outsider* what the specific strategy of a specific company is, and evaluating the effectiveness of a specific strategy.

Andrews argued that careful examination of the behavior of a company will reveal what its strategy is. As an illustration, he cited the analysis of a business policy student of the strategy of Heublein on the basis of a case written about the company.[22] Andrews also proposed nine criteria for the evaluation of a corporate strategy which he stated in question form.[23]

E. *Applying the Business Policy Framework to the Overseas Chinese*

My use of historical analysis rejected the hypothesis of the Trader Tradition for the success of the Overseas Chinese. In addition, historical analysis has validated the existence of three independent variables which can be responsible for the success of the overseas Chinese. All three of them were uniquely present in the region and among the Overseas Chinese:

1. *The transformation of the economy of the region,* first under the colonial rule of the European powers which brought the overseas Chinese to the ASEAN region in the first place and later under the independent governments which pursued economic development policies which created the economic opportunities the Overseas Chinse could exploit;

2. *The status of the Overseas Chinese as Chinese and as immigrants* provided the more powerful motivation for exploiting the opportunities presented by the transformation of the economy of the region as compared to any other distinguishable group (i.e. the indigenous Malays on the one hand and the other major migrant group, the Indians on the other hand); and

3. *The social organizations and values* which the Overseas Chinese brought with them, developed, and maintained in a threatening environment provided them with a distinct competitive advantage.

Figure III-6 presents what we term as the first stage in our hypothesis formulation process.

As stated earlier, the effect of three independent variables on the economic performance of the Overseas Chinese occurs only with the

FIGURE III-6
HYPOTHESIS FORMULATION PROCESS:
STAGE ONE

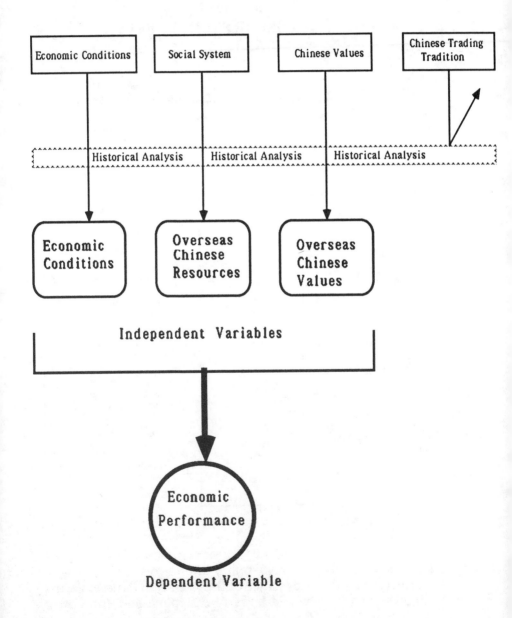

presence of all three independent variables. The absence of one in other environments has not resulted in the economic performance that we saw in the ASEAN countries. Further analysis of these three factors indicate a similarity with the four major components necessary for the formulation of corporate strategy as postulated by Andrews. Figure III-7 shows the similarity in graphic form.

FIGURE III-7
HYPOTHESIS FORMULATION PROCESS:
STAGE TWO

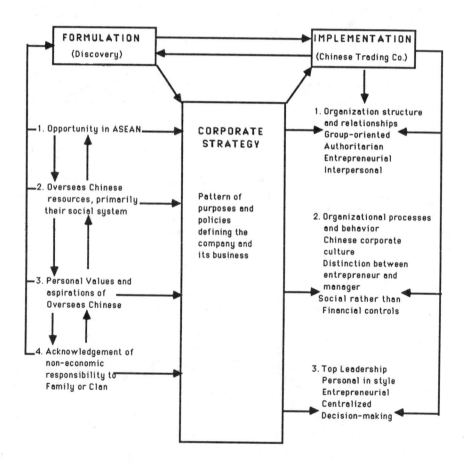

Once we adopt the business policy framework in seeking to explain the economic performance of the overseas Chinese, we are then able to tap into a whole body of discipline and conceptual frameworks. My hypothesis is that the application of this body of knowledge to the question of the economic performance of the overseas Chinese shall enable us to explain:

1. the transformation of the overseas Chinese from coolie laborers to successful entrepreneurs;
2. variations in the performance of the overseas Chinese in specific industries;
3. the alternative strategies pursued by the overseas Chinese in each of the ASEAN countries; and
4. the structure and operation of the organization chosen by the Overseas Chinese to implement their business strategies: The Chinese Trading Company.

In his book entitled *Competitive Advantage: Creating and Sustaining Superior performance,* Michael Porter outlines three generic strategies for achieving above-average performance in an industry: **cost leadership, differentiation and focus.**[24] (Figure III-5)

Based on this strategy framework, we could argue that the initial strategy adopted by the Overseas Chinese was one of **cost leadership.** Coolie labor, due to its many abuses provided the cheapest labor and thus a competitive advantage. But cost leadership under these conditions was not sustainable. Competition in the form of alternative cheaper labor sources arose. Thus in British Malaya, the Indians were brought in while in Indonesia, Javanese workers from the crowded island of Java were brought to Sumatra. Moreover, the reforms introduced to correct the grave abuses of the coolie trade also raised the cost of coolie labor. At the other end of the spectrum, the European colonial powers were continuously introducing cost-saving technologies, i.e. steam engines, electricity, specialized equipment which slowly eroded the cost advantage of coolie labor. Within this framework, it could be argued that the shift of the overseas Chinese from coolie labor to entrepreneurship was dictated, not so much by *business acumen as by economic necessity.*[25]

The business policy framework could then explain why the Overseas Chinese were more successful in some fields rather than in others. There is some historical documentation for such a disparity in economic performance.

The overseas Chinese through their cheap labor controlled tin mining in British Malaya up to the 1920s. In 1920, 64 per cent of the tin mines were operated by the Chinese, compared with 36 per cent by the Europeans. But with the introduction of modern dredging technology by the Europeans, the Chinese lost their dominance in the industry in the 1930s. In 1938, the proportion was reversed, the Europeans operated 67 per cent of the mines while the Chinese were reduced to 33 per cent.[26]

On the other hand the overseas Chinese successfully met the challenge posed by the introduction of Western technology in rice milling in Thailand. In 1858, Westerners introduced the first steam rice mill in Thailand. By 1867, there were five Western-owned steam rice mills making inroads in the industry. But the Chinese quickly converted to the new technology and by 1912, only three of the country's fifty steam rice mills were owned by the Westerners.[27]

The independent variables can now be refined to explain why the Malay Chinese could not completely adopt tin mining technology while the Thai Chinese could adopt rice milling technology and did. The Malay Chinese in tin mining were not as successful as the Thai Chinese in rice milling.

In tin mining, the competitive advantage of the Chinese was based on cost leadership. When technology challenged the basis for that leadership, the Chinese position in the tin mining industry collapsed. In rice milling, the competitive strategy of the Chinese was based on their rice collection and distribution network (a differentiation strategy). Technology did not challenge the basis of Chinese leadership in that industry and could even be used to strengthen the basis for Chinese leadership in the industry.

In the succeeding chapters, I shall endeavor to prove that the business policy hypothesis offers the most credible explanation for the transformation of coolie laborers into successful entrepreneurs by postulating multi-level strategies which coolie laborers could adopt and then discard as they become more and more successful. Figure III-8 presents how a multi-level strategy would look.

The previous business policy hypothesis was refined by varying the levels of resources available to the Chinese entrepreneurs. The business policy hypothesis could also be differentiated by varying the economic environment under which the Chinese entrepreneurs would operate. Thus, using each of the ASEAN countries as a different environment, one could speculate on the alternative strategies pursued by the most successful Chinese entrepreneurs (level 4 resources). Figure III-9 shows how this would look graphically.

Finally, the business policy hypothesis can be used in presenting a systematic analysis of the strategy, structure and operations of the Chinese Trading Company. Figure III-10 shows the classic business policy framework used in describing the strategy and structure of the Chinese Trading Company.

In summary then my hypothesis is as follows:

The creation and the sustaining of superior economic performance by the Overseas Chinese firms in the ASEAN countries can be explained by (1) the discovery of a multi-level business strategy uniquely appropriate to their resources, their value-system and the environments in which they chose or were forced to operate and (2) the effective creation of a distinctive business and management organization - The Chinese Trading Company.

FIGURE III-8
HYPOTHESIS FORMULATION PROCESS:
STAGE III

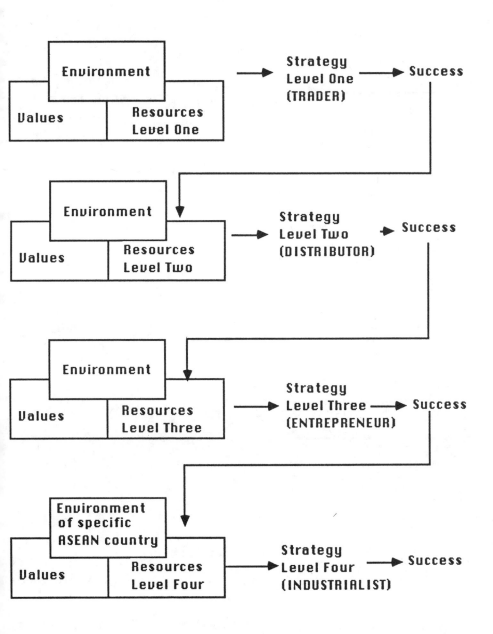

FIGURE III-9
HYPOTHESIS FORMULATION PROCESS:
STAGE FOUR

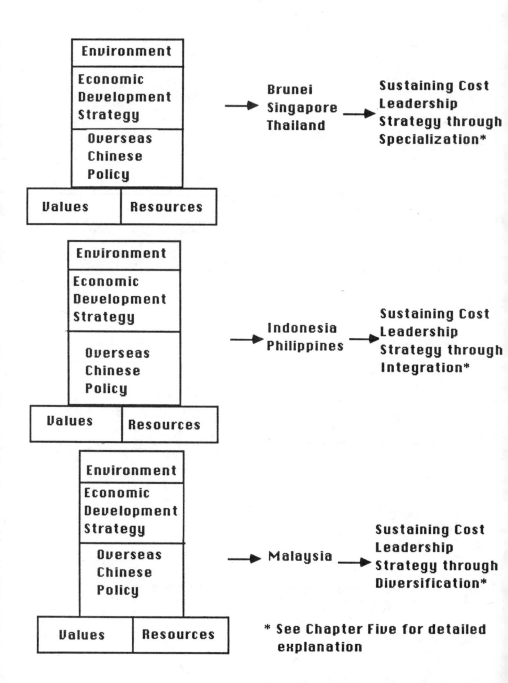

FIGURE III-10
HYPOTHESIS FORMULATION PROCESS:
STAGE FIVE

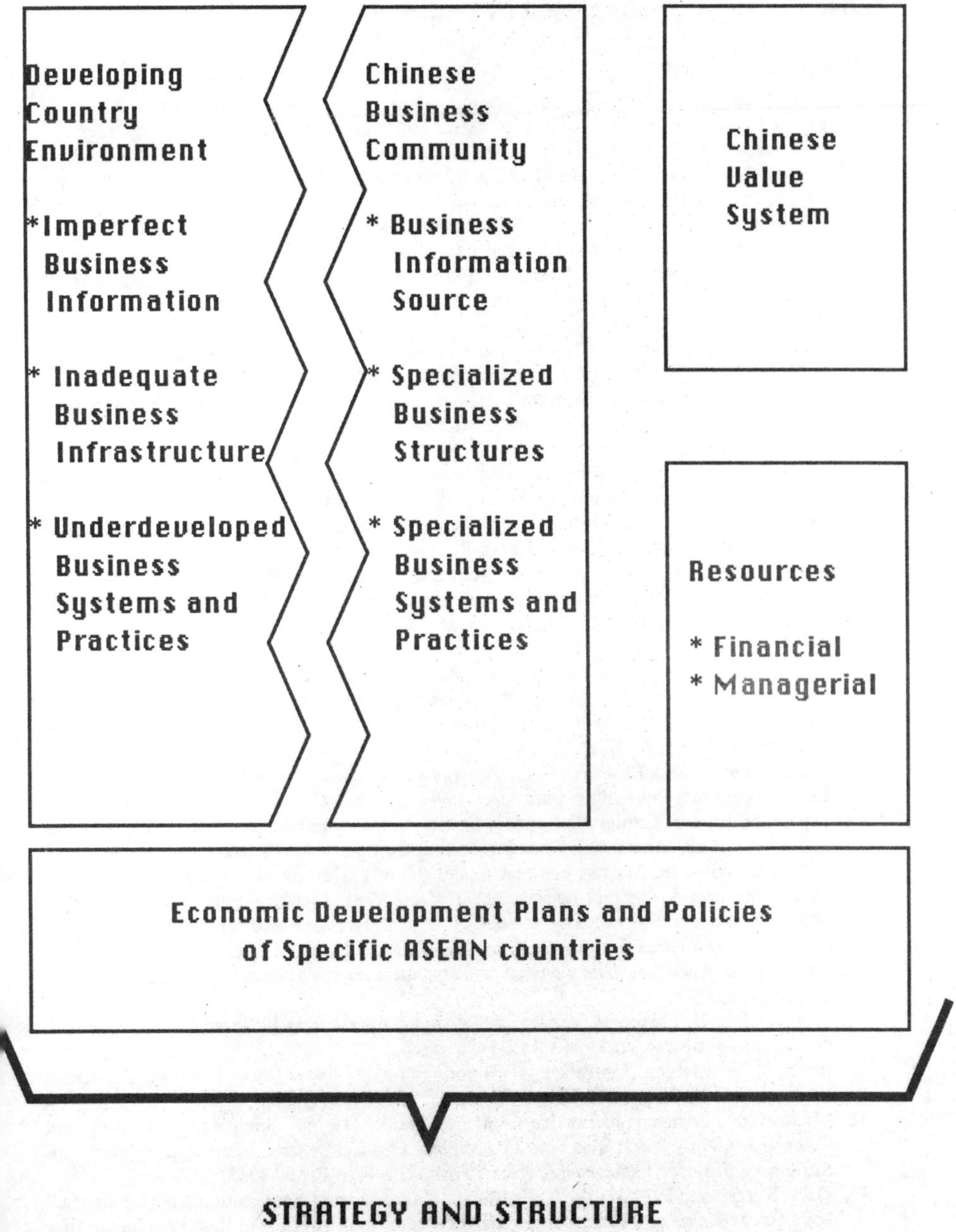

Developing
Country
Environment

*Imperfect
 Business
 Information

* Inadequate
  Business
  Infrastructure

* Underdeveloped
  Business
  Systems and
  Practices

Chinese
Business
Community

* Business
  Information
  Source

* Specialized
  Business
  Structures

* Specialized
  Business
  Systems and
  Practices

Chinese
Value
System

Resources

* Financial
* Managerial

Economic Development Plans and Policies
of Specific ASEAN countries

STRATEGY AND STRUCTURE

E. *Validating the Hypothesis*

The above hypothesis can be validated by piecing together the multi-level business strategies and management practices of the Chinese Trading Company from the data base cited in the first chapter. It can then be proven that they meet the criteria of an effective strategy suggested by Andrews.

NOTES

1. I would recommend two books as starting point for those who wish to do further study on the business policy framework; Charles Hofer and Dan Schendel, Strategy Formulation: Analytical Concepts (St. Paul, Minnesota: West Publishing Company,1978) and Jay Galbraithand Daniel Nathanson, Strategy Implementation: The Role of Structure and Process (St. Paul, Minnesota: West Publishing Company, 1978).

2. C. Roland Christensen et al., Policy Formulation and Administration, Ninth Edition (Homewood, Illinois: Richard D. Irwin, Inc., 1985), p. xi.

3. Kenneth R. Andrews, The Concept of Corporate Strategy Revised Edition (Homewood, Illinois: Richard D. Irwin, Inc., 1980), p. iv.

4. Ibid., pp. 18-19.

5. For example, in his book The Evolution of Management Thought, Second Edition (New York: John Wiley & Sons, 1979), Daniel A. Wren discusses the evolution of several schools of management thought – Scientific Management, Administrative Theory, Human Relations and Organizations, Management Science, etc. without discussing business policy or corporate strategy.

6. While business policy as a course was introduced in 1911, Kenneth Andrews in his book notes that there was resistance to the concept in executive seminars and that it was only in 1964 that the General Electric Company introduced a course in general mangement at its Crotonville institute. See Kenneth R. Andrews, The Concept of Corporate Strategy, Revised Edition (Homewood, Illinois: Richard D. Irwin, Inc., 1980), p. v.

7. For a description of the areas of research interest at that time, see Daniel A. Wren, The Evolution of Management Thought, Second Edition (New York: John Wiley & Sons, 1979).

8. Alfred D. Chandler, Jr., Strategy and Structure: Chapters in the History of the American Industrial Enterprise (Cambridge: The Massachusetts Institute of Technology Press, 1962).

9. Ibid., pp. 3-17.

10. Charles Hofer and Dan Schendel, Strategy Formulation: Analytical Concepts (St. Paul, Minnesota: West Publishing Company, 1978), pp. 18-19.

11. Jay Galbraith and Daniel Nathanson, Strategy Implementation: The Role of Structure and Process (St. Paul, Minnesota: West Publishing Company, 1978), pp. 26-48.

12. Oliver Williamson, Markets and Hierarchies (New York: The Free Press, 1975).

13. James Thompson, Organizations in Action (New York: McGraw-Hill, 1967).

14. Kenneth Andrews, Edmund Learned, C. Roland Christensen and William Guth, Business Policy: Text and Cases (Homewood, Illinois: Richard D. Irwin, Inc., 1965).

15. Kenneth R. Andrews, The Concept of Corporate Strategy (Homewood, Illinois: Dow-Jones-Irwin, 1971).

16. Igor H. Ansoff, Corporate Strategy: An Analytic Approach to Business Policy for Growth and Expansion (New York: McGraw Hill, 1965).

17. Bruce D. Henderson, Henderson on Corporate Strategy (New York: The New American Library, Inc., 1982), pp. 168-171.

18. Michael E. Porter, Competitive Strategy: Techniques for Analyzing Industries and Competitors (New York: The Free Press, 1980) and Competitive Advantage: Creating and Sustaining Superior Performance (New York: The Free Press, 1985).

19. D. W. Karger and F. A. Malik, "Long-Range Planning and Organizational Performance," Long-Range Planning, December 1975. For researches in support of their conclusion that

formalized approaches do result in superior performance, see Stanley Thune and Robert House, "Where Long Range Planning Pays Off," *Business Horizons*, August 1970, and Joseph O. Eastlack and Philip R. McDonald, "CEO's Role in Corporate Growth," *Harvard Business Review*, May/June 1970.

20. Leslie W. Rue and Robert M. Fulmer, "Is Long-Range Planning Profitable?" *Academy of Management Proceedings*, Boston, August 1973.
21. Bruce R. Scott, John W. Rosenblum and Audrey T. Sproat, *Case Studies in Political Economy: Japan 1854-1977* (Boston: Division of Research, Harvard Business School, 1980), pp. 7-8. Some development economists, of course argue that the studies of Scott et al. proceeded from previous concepts of a country's development policies which were already quite established.
22. Andrews, *The Concept of Corporate Strategy, Revised Edition*, pp. 21-22.
23. Ibid., pp. 36-42.
24. Porter, *Competitive Strategy: Techniques for Analyzing Industries and Competitorn*, pp. 34-46.
25. It may be inquired as to why the Chinese did not just accept their fate and acquiesce to lower pay. It must be noted that the Chinese had greater economic motivation than the natives. They went to work in the tin mines for economic reasons, they needed to accumulate savings to remit and bring home, and they did not have the safety net of a community and agricultural property which the natives had. The Indians, interestingly, responded by organizing labor unions which demanded better pay from the British firms which became predominant in the tin mining industry.
26. Yuan-li Wu and Chun-hsi Wu, *Economic Development in Southeast Asia: The Chinese Dimension* (Stanford: Hoover Institution Press, 1980), p. 201. The fact that some Chinese tin mines remained would indicate that some tin mines were so small or so mined out, that the capital investment in steam-powered equipment could not be justified.
27. Skinner, *Chinese Society in Thailand: An Analytical History*, pp. 103-105.

CHAPTER IV
THE CHINESE TRADING COMPANY

A. *The Strategic Situation*

When an enterprising Chinese in any of the ASEAN countries (except in Singapore) starts to evaluate the alternative business opportunities open to him, he is immediately confronted with *three inescapable realities.*

First of all, the Chinese business community, a cultural business group of which he is a member, is a distinct and formidable resource base: a source of reliable business information, an efficient market place for capital and entrepreneurial projects, and a social organization structured to encourage and facilitate business activities.

That such a resource base exists is attested to by many observers and more scientifically documented in various case studies undertaken by sociologists[1]. The most explicit study on the use of the Chinese social system for business purposes was undertaken by Clifton A. Barton. In his paper entitled "Trust and Credit: Some Observations Regarding Business Strategies of Overseas Chinese Traders in South Vietnam," Barton stated:

> The major advantage that Chinese merchants had over Vietnamese traders in developing reputations for credit worthiness derived from the nature of Chinese social organization. The Chinese community functioned as a well organised system of information, as an arena in which businessmen carried out transactions exposed to the scrutiny of others. By participating in the various associations and gatherings which were constantly being organised in the Chinese community, a businessman had available to him the information, speculation and gossip which formed the subject matter of everyone's conversations. Much of the conversation at Chinese social gatherings centred on the financial affairs of persons not present, with everyone fully realising that his own activities would be freely discussed on occasions where he himself was absent. The task of every businessman, then, was to so conduct himself in his financial affairs as to build and preserve a reputation for trustworthy, reliable and astute behaviour.[2]

Barton then provided some quantification of this competitive advantage by collecting data on the interest rates paid by Chinese merchants as contrasted with the interest rates paid by Vietnamese merchants on various types of borrowing such as bank loans, suppliers' credit, participation in rotating credit associations and loans from friends, relatives and money lenders. Barton found that on the average Chinese merchants paid interest charges of 2–3 per cent per month while interest charges paid by Vietnamese traders averaged 4-6 per cent per month.[3]

The resource base is of course effective only under certain conditions. For one, the resource base is a competitive advantage only in competition with non-Chinese firms. Other Chinese firms also have access to this resource base. As one observer of success within the Chinese community has concluded, "Success or failure in business in the Philippine environment appears to reside in what a Chinese merchant *does* with what *all* Chinese *have* (their cultural and structural givens) as members of the Chinese merchant community."[4]

A description of the organizational structures evolved by the Chinese community to assist aspiring Chinese businessmen is provided by D. Stanley Eitzen in his article entitled, "Two Minorities: The Jews of Poland and the Chinese of the Philippines."

> Perhaps the most important single group to a Chinese business man is the local Chinese Chamber of Commerce. Each Chamber of Commerce provides a forum for discussion, collects and disseminates information about trade conditions, investigates and guarantees the credentials of Chinese business men, settles disputes, conducts research, provides machinery for group action, and acts as a lobby and pressure group to promote the interests of the Chinese in their dealings with the Philippine government officials. Money is collected through the local Chamber for charity work, hospitals, cemeteries, social clubs, and especially the financing of Chinese schools. Chinese businessmen also seek protection through such trade organizations as the Philippine Chinese Hardware Association, Chinese Groceries Association, and the Philippine Manila Chinese Sari Sari Store Association. At present the larger trade associations and 120 Chambers of Commerce are united in the Federation of Chinese Chambers of Commerce to present a single cohesive front and facilitate business contacts in all the provinces.[5]

The second business reality for the entrepreneurial-minded Chinese is that he must look **outside** the Chinese business community for his business opportunities. Not only is that the arena where his access to the Chinese business community is a distinct competitive advantage but most importantly *this is where most of the opportunities exist.* After all, despite their purchasing power, the Chinese constitute only about five per cent of the population, the rest being the indigenous population. Moreover, the government market (including state-owned enterprises) which, in the ASEAN countries, constitutes as much as 30 per cent of the economic sector, is, with the sole exception of Singapore, not controlled by the Overseas Chinese.

The third business reality is that in going outside the Chinese business community to exploit those opportunities, the Chinese entrepreneur must necessarily operate in an environment which places no premium (except in the restaurant industry) on his Chinese identity. In fact, the Chinese businessman must expect a distinct preference for his non-Chinese competitors not only with respect to the official policies of the government but also with respect to the market (which is non-Chinese) that he intends to serve.

In summary then, the strategic goal of the Overseas Chinese businessmen from the budding entrepreneur to the successful industrialist, is to devise or discover a strategy by which to exploit the business opportunities that exist in the general economic environment by bringing to bear his distinct competitive advantage (membership in the Chinese business community) while at the same time neutralizing the public policies favoring his non-Chinese competitors and inducing the market to disregard its aversion to alien businessmen.[6]

B. *The Concept of Operation*

The entry strategy eventually devised or discovered by the Overseas Chinese and replicated as the generic strategy of budding entrepreneurs was based on two economic insights:

1) In a developing country, opportunities are generated primarily because of imperfect information (prices of products and commodities vary significantly between local communities); inadequate transportation (even if differences in prices for the same product or commodity are known, arbitraging the price differentials is difficult because of the cost and difficulty of moving goods); and the lack of mechanisms for smoothing these fluctuations in prices in different places and at different times (limited warehousing facilities, limited financing alternatives and no futures market).

2) In a developing country, therefore, there is a great demand for people and organizations who will perform the function of what economists call "intermediation."

The concept of operation of the Overseas Chinese businessman therefore is to perform the intermediation role by linking the different economic units in the general environment through the Chinese business community. This concept is illustrated in Figure IV-1.

Elaborating on the concept of intermediation one can examine in detail how such intermediation operates in the importation and distribution of foreign goods. The foreign supplier usually demands payment in cash while only the final consumer is expected to pay cash (credit cards are not widespread in developing countries). Because of the considerable time lag and distances to be traversed in the transfer of the goods from the foreign supplier to the final

Figure IU-1

THE CONCEPT OF OPERATION

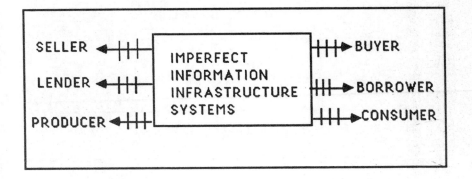

DEVELOPING COUNTRY ENVIRONMENT

CHINESE RESOURCE BASE

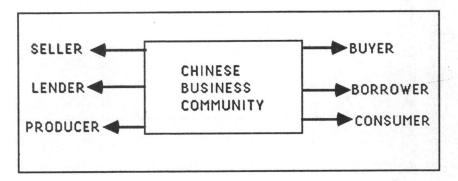

CONCEPT OF OPERATION

consumer, a considerable amount of intermediation is necessary. This intermediation process can be and is done more efficiently through the Chinese business community[7]. A Chinese importer *pays cash* to the foreign supplier and *sells the goods on credit* to a Chinese wholesaler. The Chinese wholesaler in turn sells the goods on credit to a Chinese retailer. The Chinese retailer sells the goods for cash to

FIGURE IV-2
CHINESE INTERMEDIATION

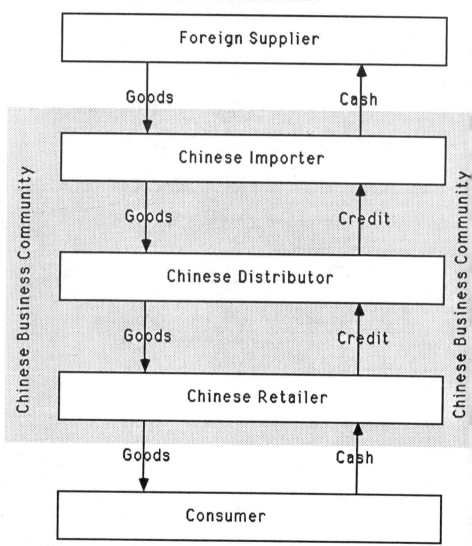

the final consumer (majority of whom are non-Chinese). This process is illustrated in Figure IV-2.

In the case of individual Chinese seeking to engage in business, their initial operation is usually in the retailing or purchasing stage. Initial involvement in the peripheral operations of retailing or purchasing usually allows them to start with a small or borrowed capital, operate on a shoestring basis, and learn the business from the ground up.

The same process of intermediation can of course be undertaken by non-Chinese organizations. In fact, attempts have been made by both the private (business groups) and public sector (government corporations) to replicate the process. That they have been less successful than the Chinese can be attributed less to their inherent inefficiency (at least for the private business groups) than to the entry strategy of the Chinese.

C. *The Entry Strategy*

Having a more efficient intermediation process creates economic surplus for the economy as a whole. The strategic decision faced by the Chinese entrepreneurs is how to allocate that surplus. There are really two extreme alternatives. One is to retain all the surplus for oneself and the other is to pass on all the surplus to the consumer.

There is some evidence that the other minority group, the Indians, sought to develop a strategy aimed at retaining most of the surplus[8]. There is considerable evidence that local business groups blessed with a similar windfall due to government support and subsidy have, to the distress of economic planners, also chosen to retain the surplus[9]. This is understandable given that the windfall is based on that most fleeting of business assets—political favor.

The Chinese entry strategy is based on passing most of the surplus to the market.

This strategic decision is not based on altruistic motives. There is some evidence that such a strategy has resulted in greater profits. The most persuasive of such evidence is the study of Hicks and Redding on the top 259 Philippine corporations. In their paper entitled "Culture and Corporate Performance in the Philippines: The Chinese Puzzle," Hicks and Redding contrast the financial performance of the Chinese firms with the non-Chinese firms. (Incidentally the Chinese entry strategy suggested here would explain the Chinese Puzzle stated in the paper.) Financial statistics on the Chinese firms as contrasted with the non-Chinese firms are presented in the following Table IV-1.

Hicks and Redding note that the sample of non-Chinese firms must be evaluated with some awareness of the presence of American firms in the non-Chinese firms. Their presence affects the sample in two ways. For one, the American firms (sales of P 7.619 billion for only 3 firms) produced higher average sales for the non-Chinese firms as compared to the Chinese firms (P286.43 million versus P228.28). Without the American firms, the average for the non-Chinese firms goes down to P110.54 million. This bias can be corrected through the use of ratios.

Table IV-1
Financial Statistics on the Commercial Sector
Top 259 Philippine Companies
1980
(Million Pesos)

Financial Statistic	Average Chinese n = 33	Average non-Chinese n = 40
Sales[a]	228.28	286.43
Assets	55.96	157.32
Equity	14.03	48.09
Gross Margin	20.77	40.39
Net Income	2.05	7.34

Source: G. L. Hicks and S. G. Redding, "Culture and Corporate Performance in the Philippines: The Chinese Puzzle," in *Essays in Development Economics in Honor of Harry T. Oshima*, page 209.
Based on an earlier and more detailed version of the paper where the number of Chinese firms were stated at 32 and the non-Chinese firms at 42.

Another bias, however must be corrected by the use of another ratio. The financial statistics were drawn from financial statements submitted for tax purposes. Since the American firms are considered to have less flexibility in underestimating their income as compared to the Chinese and Philippine firms, there is considerable basis for disregarding the net income figures. Thus Hicks and Redding in their study used the gross profit rather than the net income as the basis for evaluating the performance of the Chinese firms as compared to the non-Chinese firms. I propose to do the same.

When we compare the gross return on equity (gross profit/ equity), we find a significant variation: *148.04 per cent for the Chinese firms compared to 83.99 per cent for the non-Chinese firms.* Moreover, this is in sharp contrast to the gross margin on sales: *9.1 per cent for the Chinese firms compared to 14.1 per cent for the non-Chinese firms.*

The difference in these financial statistics can be explained by two factors. The lower gross margin on sales (gross profit/sales) of the Chinese firms is more than offset by a **greater turnover** of assets (sales/assets): *4.08 times for the Chinese firms as compared to 1.82 times for the non-Chinese firms* and by the **higher leverage** on debt (debt/equity): *2.99 times for the Chinese firms as compared to 2.27 times for the non-Chinese firms.*

The greater turnover can be explained by the lower gross margin that the Chinese firms are willing to accept while the greater leverage can be explained by the easier access to credit of the Chinese firms. The greater turnover is of course a much greater factor than the leverage. Table IV-2 presents the financial ratios while Figure IV-3 is an attempt to relate the ratios to other ratios.

Table IV-2
Financial Ratios on the Commercial Sector
Top 259 Philippine Companies
1980

Financial Ratio	Chinese	non-Chinese
Return on Equity (net income/equity)	14.61 %	16.79 %
Gross Return on Equity (gross profit/equity)	148.04 %	83.99 %
Debt Leverage (debt/equity)	2.99 x	2.27 x
Gross Return on Asset (gross profit/asset)	37.12 %	25.67 %
Gross Margin on Sales (gross profit/sales)	9.1 %	14.1 %
Asset Turnover (sales/assets)	4.08 x	1.82 x
Collection Period	27.0 days	54.8 days
Inventory Level	6.4 days	25.8 days

Source: G. L. Hicks and S. G. Redding, "Culture and Corporate Performance in the Philippines: The Chinese Puzzle," in *Essays in Development Economics in Honor of Harry T. Oshima*, page 209.

Figure IV-3
Comparative Financial Performance

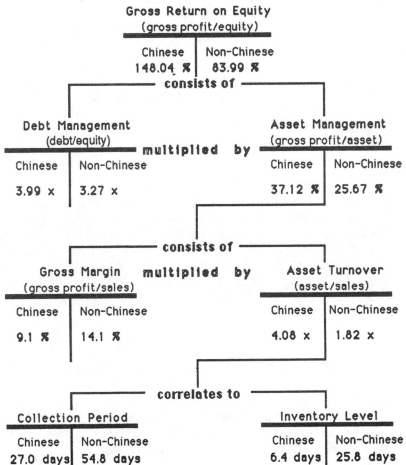

Gross Return on Equity
(gross profit/equity)

Chinese	Non-Chinese
148.04 %	83.99 %

consists of

Debt Management
(debt/equity) — multiplied by — Asset Management
(gross profit/asset)

Chinese	Non-Chinese		Chinese	Non-Chinese
3.99 x	3.27 x		37.12 %	25.67 %

consists of

Gross Margin — multiplied by — Asset Turnover
(gross profit/sales) (asset/sales)

Chinese	Non-Chinese		Chinese	Non-Chinese
9.1 %	14.1 %		4.08 x	1.82 x

correlates to

Collection Period Inventory Level

Chinese	Non-Chinese		Chinese	Non-Chinese
27.0 days	54.8 days		6.4 days	25.8 days

Having provided indications of the financial results of such an entry strategy as well as examining in financial terms how such financial results have been achieved, I now propose to detail the strategic factors which could explain the financial ratios and results.

First of all, the strategy of passing on the surplus to the consumer, as predicted by economic theory, would remove from the marketplace the less efficient (or less subsidized) businesses, thus leaving the field to the Chinese entrepreneurs. For example, in the case study on Vietnam, the Chinese merchants, with their competitive advantage in interest rates (an average of 2.5 per cent per month) over the Vietnamese traders, chose to maintain the gross margin for rice at a thin level of 2-5 per cent (adjusted monthly) and so eliminate most of the Vietnamese traders whose interest rates ranged from 4-6 per cent per month.[10]

Secondly, lower prices would counteract whatever negative feelings may exist for the alien trader among the consuming public, i. e., patriotic Americans induced to buy cheaper Japanese cars. L. A. Peter Gosling, in his paper entitled, "Chinese Crop Dealers in Malaysia and Thailand: The Myth of the Merciless Monopsonistic Middleman," concludes:

> Almost all studies of Chinese middlemen are impressed by their efficiency, relatively low profit margins and fairness. Many farmers share this view, preferring to use Chinese crop dealers rather than government-sponsored cooperatives or local crop dealers. In Thailand, several studies have found that between 70 per cent and 80 per cent of farmers are satisfied with the Chinese-dominated marketing system and believe the prices to be acceptable and the dealers to be fair.[11]

Thirdly, the low-margin/high-turnover strategy masks the enormous profits that are possible under this strategy. The widespread tendency of most casual business observers is to focus solely on the gross margin on sales without realizing that the turnover contributes just as significantly to the return on equity.

This significant distinction escapes even non-business scholars. In the same paper Gosling argues that the profits of crop dealers were not "handsome".

> Usher, in his study of Thai rice marketing, gives an example of a dealer who makes 1.5 per cent profits, while the farmer receives 79 per cent of the final sales price. The Chulalongkorn Social Research Study states that the farmers get 72.19 per cent of what the consumers finally pay for rice and that all the middlemen, including the crop dealers, wholesalers and retailers, share 12.05 per cent of the final retail sale price of rice. This latter statistic agrees with Purcal's study of the Malayan rice industry in 1962, in which all farmers receive 77.4 per

cent of the final retail sales price, mills 11.23 per cent, with all middlemen and transport costs amounting to 11.37. Of this, the wholesaler and retailer take 9.36 per cent, transport another .38 per cent, while the crop dealers receive only 1.63 per cent, rather close to Usher's estimate.

These are not handsome profit margins for dealers and are far below what is considered a minimum commission or margin for crop dealers in other parts of the world.[12]

Given this conclusion, Gosling explains the evident economic prosperity of the crop dealers to cheating (manipulation of quality standards, weights and measures) and interest on credit operation (which he later admits is included in the dealer margin).

The more accurate explanation of course is that the share of the farmer and the share of the crop dealer in the final retail price of rice are in *no way comparable*. That this is so becomes evident when we ask how many farmers will share the 79 per cent and how many crop dealers will share in the 1.5 per cent. More technically, the low margin of the crop dealer is more than compensated for by the higher turnover. In the case of the crop dealer his faster turnover can be explained by two factors. Firstly, the crop dealer does business with many farmers. Secondly, he has a much shorter production cycle.

Using the figures cited by Gosling, we could argue thus: When a farmer sells to a crop dealer, he gets 79 per cent of the retail value of the rice. For the farmer, that is all he gets. For the crop dealer while it may be true that he gets only 1.5 per cent from a single farmer, he gets the same commission from several farmers. He could, for example look to getting a total of 150 per cent from 100 farmers. Moreover, for the farmer to receive that 79 per cent, he would have to work on his farm for about four months (120 days) while the crop dealer would probably have to work for only a month to get the 150 per cent. Thus, it would not be unusual for a crop dealer getting only 1.5 per cent on sales to generate gross revenues which can be easily eight times that of the rice farmer.

The low-margin/high-turnover strategy also dictates where the opportunities for adopting such a strategy are abundant:
1) In the commodity industries where there is the greatest sensitivity in price, where large volumes of transactions are possible and where no identification of the product or commodity with the producer or distributor is necessary. Interestingly, the other industries which share the same characteristics like the securities or currency markets are not fully developed in the developing countries. However, as will be discussed later, the structure and management practices of the Chinese trading company bear the closest resemblance to the brokerage houses and investment banks.

2) In the distribution or collection function within the industries where there are numerous producers and buyers. This is the stage where the volume and turnover are the greatest. This is illustrated in Figure IV-4.

FIGURE IU-4
THE CHINESE FIRM IN THE INDUSTRY CHAIN

Numerous Producers

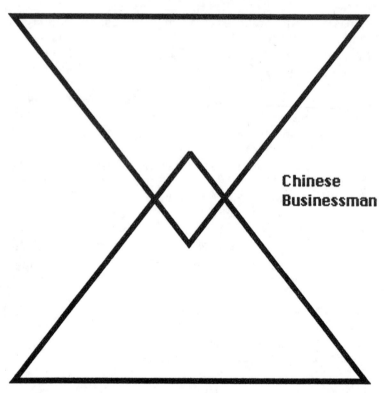

Chinese
Businessman

Numerous Consumers

Lastly the entry strategy lays the foundation for the succeeding strategy aimed at sustaining and even increasing superior economic performance.

D. *The Basic Structure of the Basic Strategy*

Assuming that the budding Chinese entrepreneur we cited has settled on the business and strategy which we have outlined above, he must now tackle the structure of the instrument of that strategy: the Chinese trading company.[13] Organizationally, the structure is quite simple. The Chinese entrepreneur is the sole owner and manager and makes all the managerial decisions. He deals with both his suppliers and his buyers, his debtors and his creditors. His main managerial concerns are financial controls (no pilferage of goods or cash by employees) and financial information (are we profitable or not?).

As a small businessman in a developing economy, the Chinese businessman cannot and probably prefers not to employ the Western double-entry type of accounting. There is considerable evidence that such accounting systems were not available in the ASEAN countries before the advent of the personal computer.

In a study conducted for the Ford Foundation in 1973-76 and later published in a book entitled *Accounting Systems in Third World Countries,* Adolf Enthoven conducted a survey of the status of the accounting profession in four Southeast Asian Countries: Indonesia, Malaysia, Philippines and Thailand. One of his more surprising findings is the great variance in the number of Certified Public Accountants in these countries. Table IV-3 presents his estimate as well as comparable statistics in other countries.

Table IV-3
Comparative Number of Certified Public Accountants
Selected Countries

Country	Number of CPAs	Number of CPAs per 100,000
Indonesia, 1975	800	0.61
Malaysia, 1975	450	3.75
Philippines, 1975	30,000	71.43
Thailand, 1975	2,800	6.67
United States, 1957	39,123	22.88
United States, 1977	179,500	83.49
United Kingdom, 1973	79,647	142.23
Italy, 1973	11,458	20.46
France, 1973	10,029	18.92
Hongkong, 1975	900	20.27

Sources: Adolf Enthoven, *Accounting Systems in Third World Economies* (Amsterdam: North-Holland Publishing Company, 1977), pp. 219, 295, 310, 320 and 331; Michael Lafferty, *Accounting in Europe,* (Cambridge: Woodhead-Faulkner Ltd., 1975) pp. 26, 202 and 267; and Gary Previts and Barbara Mesino, *A History of Accounting in America,* (New York: John Wiley & Sons, 1979), p. 305.

If the Chinese accounting system is not the Western double-entry accounting system, then what is the Chinese accounting system? My personal introduction to the Chinese accounting system was due to the insistence of a Chinese businessman that *kapag hindi tanggap, hindi kita, kapag hindi bayad, hindi utang* (No income is realized until it is received, no debt recognized until it is paid).[14] I could understand the first part which stressed that income be recognized on an "as received" basis. After all, such a practice is resorted to as a matter of prudent policy by companies which have low collection efficiencies (i.e. telegram and telegraph companies). What I could not comprehend was the statement that debt is recognized only when it is paid. Upon further reflection, one realizes that the only time that debt enters into a cash flow statement is *when it is paid*. Furthermore, one could argue that all expenses are a form of debt. The saying of the Chinese businessman, stated in an admirable economy of words, is that the accounting system is a *Cash-Flow System*. The Chinese system, therefore, *trades sophistication for simplicity*. Moreover, the Chinese evolved non-financial systems which compensated for the advantage in sophistication of the Western financial system.

The Chinese financial system (Cash Flow) lacks the sophistication of the Western financial system (Income Statement and Balance Sheet) in three major areas: **financial controls, credit management, and financial reporting**.

Whereas in the Western Financial System the double-entry concept allows continuous balancing and checking, the Chinese Financial System provides no such mechanism for continuous balancing and continuous checking. For example under the double-entry system, the receipt of cash requires a corresponding and equal entry so that the balance sheet will be balanced. In the cash flow system, the receipt of cash is just recorded as a cash receipt without any corresponding and equal changes in the cash disbursement records.

There are two alternative control systems designed to solve this inherent weakness of the Cash-Flow System. One approach favored by governments still using the Cash-Flow System is to scrutinize all transactions several times and by several individuals even to the extent of conducting pre-audits (one of the major causes of government red tape). The other alternative is to centralize all cash receipts and cash disbursements with a very few individuals who can be completely trusted. Given the Chinese value system, it comes as no surprise that the second approach is strongly favored by the Chinese businessman. It may be argued that the centralization of the cash and inventory management carries the consequent risk of heavy reliance on a few individuals who can be trusted. In response, the Chinese businessman could argue that individuals with such personal loyalty and trust are available in abundance within the Chinese family and kinship system. For under the Chinese social system, any misdeed by an individual means "loss of face" for family and clan.

The family and clan can be expected to exert the necessary social pressure on the individual not to betray the trust of the manager.

Credit management under a cash-flow system requires an alternative system. For one, the tools of credit analysis based on the availability of reliable financial statements (collection period, inventory level, debt coverage, etc.) are all inoperative. Credit within the Chinese business is a matter of personal references and guarantees.

Extension of credit to non-Chinese firms is based on a different approach.[15] The basic premise of the Chinese credit evaluation system is that any businessman worth his salt should have some access to cash, the only question being its cost. It is therefore a common practice for Chinese businessmen to offer a substantial cash discount when a non-Chinese businessman first asks for credit. For example, if a non-Chinese businessman were to ask for a 30-day credit on a specific purchase, a Chinese supplier may make a counter-offer of a five per cent cash discount. If the non-Chinese businessman insists on the credit extension despite this offer, then the Chinese businessman rightly concludes that the non-Chinese businessman has no access to credit which charges a maximum of five per cent per month. For if he did, he would have availed himself of those alternative sources of credit and paid cash for his purchase. That he did not would indicate that he had no access to credit and therefore is a credit risk. If the non-Chinese businessman is readily able to come up with the cash, then his access to cash is proven and he will probably be extended credit the next time around.

In terms of credit documentation, the Chinese businessman piggybacks on the commercial banking system. Credit documentation is simply handled through the *issuance of postdated checks*. Credit collection is a simple matter of depositing the checks in the bank as they fall due. Credit extension is done simply by exchanging one postdated check for another. The credit rating of a business man is simple to assess:
1) Do the checks that he issues bounce?
2) Does he request that the postdated checks he issues not be deposited?
3) How long has he been issuing bounce-free postdated checks?

There are significant advantages to this type of credit documentation. For example, in settling business disputes among Chinese businessmen, the Chinese Chamber of Commerce simply relies on the bounced check as the basis (*prima facie evidence* in legal terminology) for its arbitration decisions. For another, postdated checks from reputable Chinese firms can be traded in the market at a discount. Thus, to check the credit rating of a Chinese firm, one merely has to know at what rate his postdated checks are being discounted in the market. Lastly, the credit system tends to promote greater credit consciousness. A Filipino banker explains why this is so. Filipino borrowers who can claim good credit standing on the basis of conventional credit analysis are more prone to ask for extensions and delay payments. Chinese borrowers whose credit standing is based solely on the reputation for meeting postdated check obligations are more religious about meeting their obligations.[16]

In terms of determining the profitability of their firms, the Chinese business community provides an interesting study of how social customs can be enlisted to serve business ends. During the Chinese New Year, the Chinese business community (and the Chinese community in general) liquidate all their debts. This business practice achieves several objectives.

Through this practice, Chinese businessmen relying on the Cash-Flow System, determine their profitability. After all, if all income is received and all debt is paid by the Chinese New Year, what remains in cash, inventory or fixed assets must be profits. (More accurately equity, the difference from one Chinese New Year to the next is profit.)

This widespread periodic liquidation of debts has been observed by several scholars.[17] An indirect but more compelling evidence is the number of financial scandals that occur at this time of the year. For example, in the Philippines and in Indonesia, the disappearance of prominent Chinese businessmen occurred before the Chinese New Year and was confirmed after the Chinese New Year when they were unable to meet their financial obligations.[18]

E. *Succeeding Strategy I : Proctor and Gamble Distributor*

Once the entry strategy of low-margin/high-turnover succeeds in capturing a substantial share of the market for the Chinese trader, he acquires both the bread-and-butter line to cover his operating expenses and to lay the groundwork for the next level of business growth. Given his large market share, the trader usually has five alternative strategies:

1) Integrate forward into the distribution system (from dealer to mass merchandiser).
2) Integrate backward into the distribution system.
3) Integrate backward into production.
4) Expand into other product lines.
5) Diversify into other business activities.

Integrating forward into mass merchandising is an alternative open primarily to Chinese traders operating in the big cities (i.e. Central Department Store in Bangkok and Makati Supermarket in Manila). Moreover, retail trade laws restricting Chinese participation are not based on volume of sales but on selling to end consumers. For example, in the Philippines, mass merchandisers like the American oil companies were deemed involved in retailing and so had to transfer their retailing operations to Filipinos. Integrating backward into the distribution system is possible but is an alternative to only a few. Moreover, integrating forward would bring the Chinese trader into business competition with bigger and more efficient Chinese traders. Thus while this alternative exists, it is available only to the few and the sharpest of traders. An indication of the pyramidic structure of the distribution system may be gleaned from a study of rubber dealers in Malaysia by Janet T. Landa.

Table IV-4
Number of Dealers in West Malaysia
1967

Trade Level	No. of Dealers	% of Total
Licensed Exporter	63	3.0
Second Level Dealer	677	30.0
First Level Dealer	1,500	67.0
Total		2,240 100.0

Source: Janet T. Landa, "The Political Economy of the Ethnically Homogeneous Chinese Middleman Group in Southeast Asia: Ethnicity and Entrepreneurship in a Plural Society," in Linda Y. C. Lim and L. A. Peter Gosling, *The Chinese in Southeast Asia: Ethnicity and Economic Activity*, page 110.

For those Chinese traders who are able to integrate forward, the increased volume of their business transactions allows them to pursue activities involving economies of scale. Such areas for economies of scale include warehousing, in-house transportation, and some processing (i. e. rice milling). From these more successful traders would be drawn the entrepreneurs and industrialists who will be discussed in succeeding chapters.

Integrating backward into production (i. e. rice farming) is another alternative. In general, however, this alternative usually places the Chinese trader in an industry function where his competitive advantage cannot be brought to bear and where he must compete in terms of production efficiency rather than trading proficiency. Exceptions do occur, however. A notable example is the market gardeners in Thailand.[19]

The strategy alternative that is usually pursued by the Chinese trader is to expand into other lines. In areas where commodities are seasonal and planted in the same area, the Chinese trader usually expands by trading in other commodities. The most common practice of Chinese traders, however, is to trade in products coming from the city, in effect seeking to be dealers for companies like Proctor and Gamble, Goodyear Tire and Rubber, etc.

Under this strategy alternative, the Chinese trader completes his function as the intermediary between the dual economies of the city and the countryside. This role is illustrated in Figure IV-5.

There are several advantages to this strategy which would explain its more widespread adoption. First of all, the Chinese trader by handling the distribution of the farm inputs (fertilizer, pesticide, even household products for the farmer) from the city generates additional business from his *existing market*. His existing access to the market sharply reduces his marketing costs in terms of credit

FIGURE IV-5
THE CHINESE FIRM IN THE DUAL ECONOMY

Urban Economy

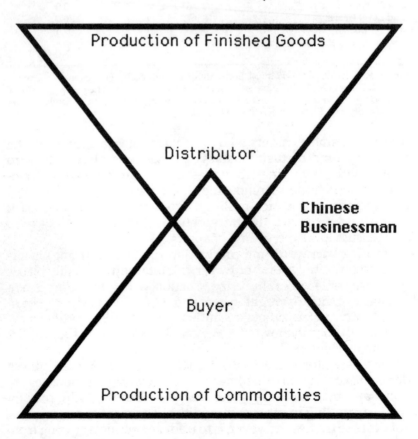

Production of Finished Goods

Distributor

Chinese Businessman

Buyer

Production of Commodities

Rural Economy

risks (paying with farm inputs for purchase of rice) and transportation costs (the trucks returning empty from the city will now be filled).

Secondly, by carrying another line and accessing another source of credit, he is effectively increasing his financial resource base. The cash that is advanced to him by the second level dealers to pay for purchases from the farmers is now available for his use when he pays the farmers in farm inputs rather than in cash.

Lastly, the potential for fuller utilization of trucks (carrying rice to the city and bringing back laundry soap to the rural area) enables the Chinese trader to buy his own trucks. This gives the Chinese trader a competitive advantage against other dealers who operate only in commodity buying or only in product distribution. (It may be argued that it would be relatively easy to copy this strategy. As will be discussed in Chapter VII, governments in the ASEAN countries have not found it easy to copy such strategy.)

The last strategy alternative of diversification into other business activities has not been fully developed. For one, success in the existing business activities precludes an active search for alternatives. When the Chinese diversify, they do so primarily into two areas: transportation and financing. Donald M. Nonini, in his paper entitled, "The Chinese Truck Transport 'Industry' of a Peninsular Malaysian Market Town," provides a case study of such a diversification.[20] It is worth nothing that in this study, 102 out of the 105 people who own and manage the thirty-four Pekan Tebu transport companies are Chinese.

The Chinese diversification into financing will be discussed more fully in Chapter V in the case studies of Bangkok Bank of Thailand and the Overseas Chinese Banking Corporation (OCBC) of Singapore. As will be noted, this diversification route is usually followed by the big-time Chinese traders.

In terms of managerial organization, the growth of the Chinese trader into this next level poses no undue pressure for substantial change. The main difference from the first level is the addition of a logistical organization such as a rice milling unit, a warehousing unit or a transport unit. This logistical organization can be handled by technically qualified professionals without impinging on the business decision-making process of the Chinese trading company. As analogy, one could cite a brokerage firm including a backroom operation (accounting unit, legal staff, or computer operators) in its organization with no substantial change in the managerial organization or practices.

F. *Succeeding Strategy II : Fresh Lanzones from Far Zamboanga*

The leap from distributor to entrepreneur can probably be best illustrated by the case of a dealer in fresh fruits in the Philippines.[21]

In the late seventies, the Philippine government established a government corporation called the Philippine Aerospace Development Corporation (PADC) to provide airfreight transportation in that island nation. One of the major destinations was the Southern Philippine city of Zamboanga (about 500 miles from Manila). The hope of the government was that with the rapid transportation of fresh fruits from the orchard farms of the province of Zamboanga to the major market of Manila, both the fresh fruit growers in Zamboanga and the consumer in Manila would benefit. The PADC was quite surprised to discover that the price of fresh lanzones in the Zamboanga fresh fruit market *actually dropped*. Further investigation revealed that a lanzones trader in Zamboanga had booked all the available space in their cargo planes. Having thus managed to obtain control of the link between Manila and Zamboanga, he then sought to obtain all arbitrage profits which flowed from this linkage. The price of lanzones dropped because the trader was dumping a substantial portion of his purchases in the Zamboanga fresh fruit market. Since the price of lanzones given to the orchard growers was based on the Zamboanga market price and not on the Manila market price, he was, in the enviable position of **buying low and selling high**.

G. The Chinese Entrepreneur

The more interesting question that the case poses is how the Chinese entrepreneur made the successful leap. Three major factors were responsible for his success: **the Chinese business framework, the business policies and practices flowing from that framework, and the Chinese Trading Company structure.**

My introduction to the Chinese deal-making occurred when I was discussing a specific business opportunity with a certain Chinese businessman.[22] His persistent question was, *Gaano katagal matutulog ang pera?* (How long will the money sleep?). From this and from a series of other questions, I have derived the Chinese business framework, which is essentially one of *pakulo* (deal-making). (This framework is shared by other ASEAN businessmen. Filipino businessmen usually start a business discussion with the question, *Ano ba ang pakulo natin?* [What deal are you working on?])

For a Chinese businessman in a business deal, cash metaphorically goes to sleep until it is transformed (awakened) into cash again, hopefully growing bigger during its period of slumber. Figure IV-6 presents a diagram of this process. (see following page)

The more technically accurate but definitely less picturesque definition of the above process is the *Cash Generation Cycle*. The type of operation is most suitable to a business opportunity which has a definite beginning and a definite end. The Western designa-

FIGURE IV-6
THE CHINESE BUSINESS FRAMEWORK

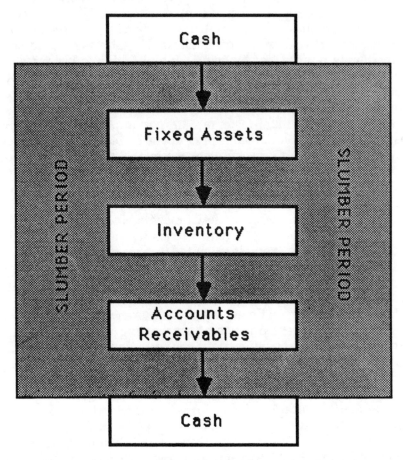

tion for this type of business operations is *Project Management* operations.

Several explanations can account for this Chinese business framework. For one the uncertain political environment may have induced in the Chinese businessman a great concern for his flexibility in liquidating his investments in a speedy manner. For another, his cash accounting system, in which overall profitability is known only at the end of the Chinese New Year, may have produced a preference for projects where profitability can be determined. Lastly, the history of the Chinese in trading in commodities which have a defined cycle may have shaped the Chinese business framework. For whatever reasons, specific business policies and practices have followed from such a business framework.

First of all, focusing on the cash-generation cycle immediately demonstrates the effect of a fast turnover. For under this framework, the period of danger is the sleeping period, where cash may never awake from its deep slumber (i.e. invested in uncollectible receivables). A willingness to trade a smaller margin for a shorter sleeping time gives rise to a turnover orientation. The Chinese businessman immediately notices that by being content with a lower price and smaller margin, he is able to sell much faster, thus shortening the slumber period. Thus he would prefer a margin of 10 per cent compared to a margin of 20 per cent knowing that he may be able to move his goods at a much faster rate and so compensate for the lower margin. (For example, if by this price cut he is able to move his goods from once a month to once a week, he is able to double his gross profit.)

Conversely, when the business deal requires an extended slumber period, the ordinary rates of returns are not acceptable. Thus, when financing is extended by the Chinese businessman, the trading gain must be of a speculative nature to justify the extended slumber period. For example, credit is extended to farmers if the produce can be purchased at harvest time when the price is at its lowest and when there is a strong likelihood that prices will rise significantly during the off-season.

Operationally, the Chinese business framework eliminates the Western management practice of segregating marketing from financing and to establishing profit centers. When a Chinese trader makes a cash advance to an Ilocano tobacco grower in the Philippines, he does not (in fact can not) segregate the income from financing the farmer, the income from warehousing the tobacco, the income from arbitraging from Ilocos to Manila, the income from tobacco distribution and the income from extending receivable financing to the tobacco manufacturer. His main concern is to generate an amount of cash at the end of the cycle sufficiently large to compensate for the sleeping time of his money.

Lastly, the more sophisticated Chinese businessmen can be expected to be involved in several deals at different stages of completion at any one time. Moreover, there may also be subdeals which can only be understood if they are components of a packaged deal. For example, a Chinese businessman may be willing to *sell some goods at a loss* simply because he considers such a subdeal as a source of financing (the cash from the sale is generated long before the accounts payable to the supplier are due), and therefore looks at the expected losses merely as financing cost.

Such business practices have had unexpected adverse consequences on non-Chinese businessmen. Appliance dealers in the Philippines have learned to their sorrow that competing with the

Chinese dealers who view appliance selling as a source of financing was a losing proposition. For the money was not made in selling the appliances (their business) but rather in taking advantage of the liberal financing terms of the appliance manufacturers and investing the money somewhere else (not their business). Subsidiaries of multinationals have also been affected. One of the competitive advantages of Western multinationals is access to low-cost credit. Thus, as part of their marketing strategy they usually provide liberal credit terms. Several tire manufacturers have found that this policy could backfire. Chinese dealers regularly take advantage of such liberal credit by "dumping" the product. For example, they purchase P100,000.00 worth of tires on a 120-day credit term. Then they turn around and sell the tires for cash forP95,000.00. The resulting loss of P5,000.00 is considered as interest expense and the P95,000.00 in cash is used in a business deal which would yield enough to cover the increased expense and provide additional income to the Chinese dealer as well. The tire companies, therefore find themselselves selling a commodity rather than a product and operating a financing company rather than a manufacturing company.

The structure organized specifically for deal-making is the Chinese Trading Company.[23] Before describing such an organization, I would like to discuss the process of deal-making. Deals have their own business logic which must be understood:

1) Deals cannot be programmed. They can only be prepared for. The economic explanation for this observation is that deals are economic activities intended to correct sudden and unexpected aberrations in the orderly working of the market place (imperfect information, gaps in the infrastructure, inconsistency in government policies, etc.);

2) Deals require immediate decision, immediate action and immediate funding. Again the economic explanation for this observation is the tendency of the market place to correct such aberrations. The time of correction may range from several years (i.e. government policies) to several minutes (i.e. foreign currency trading) but most aberrations probably last for only several months;

3) Deals which turn sour cause substantial investment in money and management; thus the key to deal-making is screening out the bad deals without also screening out the good deals;

4) The pressure and anxiety of looking for and closing a deal affects negatively one's ability to screen out bad deals as well as one's ability to negotiate favorable terms on a good deal.

The business framework of the cash-generation cycle with its emphasis on cash generation provides a competitive advantage in deal-making. As stated above, deals cannot be scheduled in advance. So the Chinese businessman must be prepared to have cash on hand or be able to raise cash at a short notice so as to take advantage of a fleeting business opportunity. (Unfortunately, this ability is fully recognized by kidnappers who usually find the Chinese the most attractive targets.)

The premium placed on cash availability is also illustrated by the common practice of some Chinese businessmen. These business-men have adopted the practice of borrowing from the bank (usually a long and tortuous process in developing countries) and then turning around and placing the *same* money in the *same* bank. For example, a Chinese businessman borrows P1,000,000.00 from a bank at an interest rate of 18 per cent per annum and then places the money in the money market department of the *same* bank at 12 per cent per annum. This may appear to be an unsound business practice as the business man obviously loses in the transaction (a negative carry of six per cent in banking terms). The rationale for such a practice is that the Chinese businessman is willing to cover the cost of the interest-differential if in so doing it increases his assurance of access to ready cash. In other words, if he has a *credit line* with a bank, the bank may at any time decide that money is tight (a common occurrence in developing countries) and so may not make the funds available when urgently needed. However, if a businessman were withdrawing his money from the bank, the bank is duty bound to lend the funds despite any liquidity problems it may have. (Multi-tiered interest rate policies by the government can make this insur-ance policy cost-free. The Chinese businessman borrows at conces-sionary rates and lends at market rates).

Within the business framework of the cash generation cycle, it is possible to define the deals which would be most attractive to a Chinese businessman:

1)   A deal which, after the process is started and the cash that is invested has already been recovered, still continues to yield cash inflows; i. e. *tubong lugao* (gravy profits); and

2)   A deal which is self-financing and therefore requires no cash outlay; i. e. *ginisa sa sariling taba* (fried in its own fat).

The Chinese Trading Company is ideally suited as a business organization for deal-making because all its activities can be conven-iently divided into two: **the deal-sustaining activities and the deal-making activities.**

The deal-sustaining activities flow from two distinct business operations:

1)   Distributorship arrangements for products and services needed in the provincial areas. A potential list would include gasoline, tires, batteries, fertilizer, pesticides, detergents, cigarettes, liq-uor, canned and package food stuff and personal care products.

This activity basically involves the movement of finished goods from the city to the rural areas;
2) Consolidation arrangements for commodities produced in the provincial areas for transport and processing to the urban centers. These commodities range from rice, rubber, copra, palm oil, sugar, fresh fruits and vegetables to handicraft products.

The role of the Chinese Trading Company as the finished goods supplier and commodities buyer of the community (mission statement in business policy terminology) is the basis for its deal-sustaining activities. These activities consist of:
1) Providing the bread and butter line. The product and commodity dealerships provide the small but steady margins which allow the Chinese Trading Company to explore and exploit business opportunities without the disconcerting pressure of trying to cover operating and living expenses.
2) Providing timely and cost-free information on possible business deals. In effect, one of the requisite steps in deal-making—information gathering—is generated in the course of trading. In production management terms, information is a by-product which is generated as part of the process and thus carries no cost.
3) Providing immediate access to cash. As stated, an important requisite of deal-making is a significant amount of cash or at least access to cash. A trading operation is ideally suited to generating substantial cash at short notice. Blessed with the advantage that supplier's credit is always easier, faster and even cheaper to obtain than bank financing, the alternative ways by which a trading company can generate cash are to:
   a) Defer payment of payables to suppliers, thus freeing cash from the collection of receivables to finance the business deal (at least temporarily);
   b) Dump inventory for cash, even at a loss;
   c) Increase purchases from suppliers and dump the additional inventory for cash, even at a loss; and
   d) Request regular clients to prepay their receivables by persuasion or by substantial discounts.

The managerial implications of adding deal-making to the basic structure of the Chinese Trading Company is for the owner-manager to assume the operating responsibility for the deal-making activities and then shift the deal-sustaining activities to a trusted relative, preferably a son. Figure IV-7 indicates how the management structure of a Chinese Trading Company would look at this level of strategy.

H.*Summary*

In summary then, my thesis is that the Overseas Chinese, operating in the developing economy of the ASEAN countries and aware of both their competitive resource, the Chinese business community

FIGURE IU-7
THE ORGANIZATIONAL CHART
THE CHINESE TRADING COMPANY

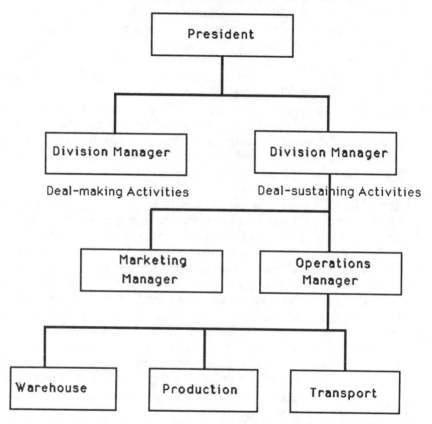

and their competitive disadvantage in seeking to serve the indigenous market, have developed a successful series of business strategies. This series of strategies is based on a low-margin/high volume strategy aimed at capturing market share. From the base of a substantial market share, the Overseas Chinese have sought to create and sustain their competitive advantage by pursuing economies of scope rather than economies of scale. As a further base for creating and sustaining their competitive advantage, the Overseas Chinese have developed a system of distinct managerial practices which draw upon their social system and customs and are at the same time consistent with the business strategy they have evolved. These strategies have three additional advantages:

1) They are generic in the sense that they can be replicated in different areas and in different commodity markets by other Chinese business men but *not* by non-Chinese businessmen.

2) They are multi-stage in the sense, that the Chinese businessman can move sequentially and logically from a simple strategy to a more sophisticated one.

3) They enable the creation of the Chinese trading company, a highly deal-oriented organization which provides both the training and the capital for Chinese entrepreneurs to become Chinese industrialists.

NOTES

1. R. J. Coughlin, *Double Identity: The Chinese in Modern Thailand* (Hongkong: Hongkong University Press, 1960), Chapter VI: Economic Organization and Interests; Maurice Freedman, *The Study of Chinese Society* (Stanford: Stanford University Press, 1979); and Linda Y. C. Lim and L. A. Peter Gosling, *The Chinese in Southeast Asia: Ethnicity and Economic Activity* (Singapore: Maruzen Asia,1983), and John T. Omohundro, *Chinese Merchant Families in Iloilo:Commerce and Kin in a Central Philippine City* (Athens, Ohio: The Ohio University Press, 1981), Chapter 3: Chinese Business Life and Chapter 4: Organizing for Business and Defense.

2. Clifton A. Barton, "Trust and Credit: Some Observations Regarding Business Strategies of Overseas Chinese Traders in South Vietnam," in Lim and Gosling, *The Chinese in Southeast Asia: Ethnicity and Economic Activity.*

3. Ibid., p. 61.

4. John T. Omohundro, "Social Networks and Business Success for the Philippine Chinese," in and Gosling, p. 67.

5. D. Stanley Eitzen, "Two Minorities: The Jews of Poland and the Chinese of the Philippines," *Jewish Journal of Sociology*, 1968, Volume 10, Number 2, pp. 221-240.

6. For summary of public policies of the ASEAN governments favoring the indigenous businessmen, see pp. 80-81 of this book.

7. As illustrated in Figure IV-1, the Chinese business community is a highly efficient business sub-sytem operating within a less efficient economic system. Therefore, transactions which are processed thru this sub-system will be less costly and time-consuming. Sources attesting to such efficiency will be cited in the succeeding notes.

8. In my interviews with several Chinese business men, one of the questions I asked was the difference between the Chinese and the Indian way of doing business in the ASEAN countries. The common reply was that while the Chinese made money from turnover, the Indians made money from financing. In other words, the Indian businessmen usually retained the surplus and chose as their competitive advantage payment for the higher priced goods (compared to the Chinese, that is) over a period of time. Such strategy, while highly effective in Burma, was not as effective as the Chinese. For one, unlike in Burma, Indians could not take over the land of the farmers. For another, the need to personally handle the collection of receivables precluded the capability to increase the volume of the business.

9. G. L. Hicks and S. G. Redding, "Culture and Corporate Performance in the Philippines:The Chinese Puzzle," in *Essays in Development Economics in Honor of Harry T. Oshima* (Manila: Philippine Institute for Development Studies, 1982).

10. Barton, "Trust and Credit: Some Observations Regarding Business Strategies of Overseas Chinese Traders in South Vietnam," in Lim and Gosling, (Singapore: Maruzen Asia, 1983), pp. 61-62.

11. Gosling, "Chinese Crop Dealers in Malaysia and Thailand: The Myth of the Merciless Monopsonistic Middleman," in Lim and Gosling, (Singapore: Maruzen Asia, 1983), p. 160.

12. Ibid., p. 139.

13. It is assumed here that the budding Chinese entrepreneur has enough capital (accumulated or borrowed) to be a dealer rather than a mere retailer or buyer. In other words, the operation is of a certain size to require the management of some people and some record keeping. For a description of a Chinese trader, see "Lo's Family Dry Goods Store: A Case Study," in John T. Omohundro, *Chinese Merchant Families in Iloilo:Commerce and Kin in a Central Philippine City* (Athens, Ohio: The Ohio University Press, 1981), pp. 169-180.

14. I wrote this up in a paper while a member of the faculty of the Asian Institute of

Management. See Victor S. Limlingan, "Chinese *Pakulo*: Project Management in an Asian Setting, " Occasional Paper No.2, *Asian Institute of Management*, July 1982. Reactions from participants in the management seminars were unanimous in confirming its accuracy. See also Omohundro, pp. 68-70.

15. I owe this description of the credit management system to a lecture by a former Chinese student.

16. I owe this description of the use of post-dated checks to a former faculty member who joined a Chinese bank in the Philippines.

17. R. J. Coughlin, *Double Identity: The Chinese in Modern Thailand* (Hongkong: Hongkong University Press, 1960), p. 124.

18. For example, in January of 1981, a prominent Filipino-Chinesebusiness man named Dewey Dee disappeared, leaving behind an estimated US$ 70 million in debt. See "Creditors Seek Philippine Executive Who Left Country Owing $70 million," *Asian Wall Street Journal*, January 30, 1981, p. 1.

19. James A. Hafner, "Market Gardening in Thailand: The Origins of an Ethnic Chinese Monopoly," in Lim and Gosling.

20. Donald M. Nonini, "The Chinese Truck Transport 'Industry' of a Peninsular Malaysian Market Town," in Lim and Gosling.

21. My source for this case was the President of the Philippine Aerospace Development Corporation.

22. Limlingan, "Chinese *Pakulo*: Project Management in an Asian Setting, " Occasional Paper No.2, *Asian Institute of Management*, July 1982.

23. I wrote this up in a paper entitled, "The Chinese Trading Company: An Organization for Opportunity Exploration and Exploitation," while a member of the faculty of the Asian Institute of Management. Reactions from participants in the management seminars were unanimous in confirming its accuracy.

CHAPTER V
THE CHINESE INDUSTRIALISTS

A.*Institutionalizing the Business Deal: Indonesia and the Philippines*

In 1952, Lea E. Williams of Harvard University wrote a paper entitled, "Chinese Entrepreneurs in Indonesia,"[1] in which he argued that the Chinese **have failed** (bold letters mine) to achieve entrepreneurship and presented facts and analysis as to why this was so. While Williams conceded that the Chinese in Indonesia were dominant in the retail and the intermediate trades, he argued that they were in no sense *entrepreneurs* as defined by Schumpeter. They were concerned merely with the exchange rather than the production of goods[2]. As to the prospects for the rise of Chinese entrepreneurs (industrialists by our definition), Williams concluded;

> This brings the question down to the present. Can the Chinese community of independent Indonesia, in the light of its past record of failure to achieve entrepreneurship, now give rise to entrepreneurs? The writer feels that **it is unlikely.**[3] (bold letters mine)

On April 7, 1983, the *Far East Economic Review* did a cover story on the Liem Group of Indonesia, hailing "the birth of a multinational".[4] In a companion article on Liem Sioe Liong (also known as Soedono Salim[5]), the magazine described Liem as a shadowy Chinese entrepreneur whose group is considered the largest private group in Indonesia, consisting of about 40 companies with a turnover of more than US$1 billion a year and an estimated workforce of 25,000. Not only is the group engaged in the traditional business of trade and distribution but also in financial services and manufacturing. In fact, the group's largest investments are in companies engaged in heavy industry and manufacturing, consisting mainly of Bogasari, a flour-milling company, which controls directly or indirectly all the country's flour mills, of Indocement, the country's largest cement producer and of Cold Rolling Mill Indonesia Utama, the country's first cold rolling steel mill. Figure V-1 presents the major components of Liem's investments in Indonesia (the offshore investments will be discussed in Chapter six).

While Liem Sioe Liong has been the most successful among the Overseas Chinese industrialists in Indonesia, he is by no means the only one. In another article[6], the *Far East Economic Review* noted the existence of Chinese industrialists in basic industries such as logging, shipping, construction and even in such traditional Indonesian industries such as *batik* cloth production, *kretek* (clove) cigarettes and *jamu* (Javanese herbal medicine). Clearly, the Chinese in Indonesia have disproven the prediction of Williams.

FIGURE U-1
THE LIEMS' ONSHORE EMPIRE

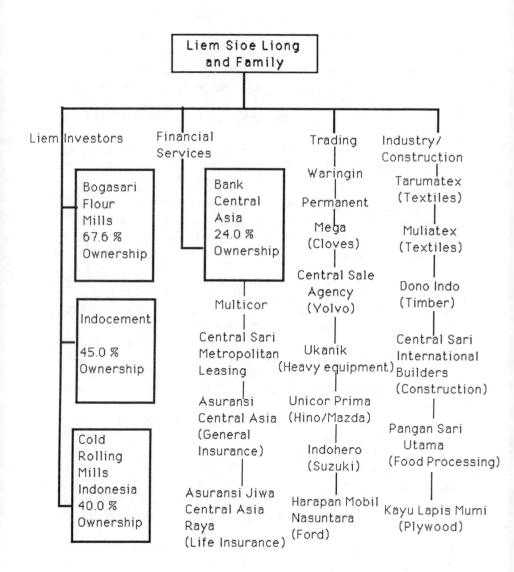

Source: *Far Eastern Economic Review*, April 7, 1983, p. 51

My objective, however is not to illustrate the perils of predicting the future but rather to use the analysis of Williams as a starting point to explain the rise of Chinese industrialists in Indonesia and the Philippines. The bases for Williams' prediction on the prospect for the rise of Chinese industrialists in Indonesia may be stated as follows:

1. The Chinese businessmen who are potential industrialists have *no incentive* to move from trading to producing. First of all, the Chinese are doing very well in trading and so would see no need to go from one lucrative business activity to an uncertain though promising business activity. Secondly, the political environment in which they have operated and expect to operate in the future *does not provide any incentive* to invest in long-term projects.

2. *Even if* the Chinese businessmen had the incentive to engage in manufacturing, long-term capital for such projects simply is not available. In the first place, the Chinese who came to Indonesia are poor and without capital. Secondly, a substantial portion of what little is saved is remitted to relatives in China, thus preventing the accumulation of capital. Thirdly, whatever little capital that is accumulated and retained in Indonesia is not recycled by being invested in the banking system. Fourthly, whatever capital is accumulated after all these obstacles is usually invested in non-productive assets (opulent houses, jewelry, consumables). Lastly, the Dutch banks prior to independence have not extended any significant long-term loans to Chinese businessmen and the banks under the Indonesian government certainly will not.

3. *Even if* the Chinese businessmen had the incentive and *even if* long-term funds were available, "the Chinese business organization was singularly unsuited to the operation of large and commercial enterprise".[7] In arguing that the Chinese business organization was *not* suitable for an industrial enterprise, Williams cited Max Weber, whose theory of the Protestant Ethic has been expanded into the Confucian Ethic by those trying to explain the economic success of the Overseas Chinese. In *The Religion of China,* Weber argued that Chinese business practices rooted in the Chinese values of family and religion would prevent the transition to rational entrepreneurial capitalism, with its structure of legal contracts and impersonal business relationships.[8]

The forces preventing the rise of Chinese industrialists were accurately identified and assessed by Williams. But the forces which encouraged the rise of Chinese industrialists were never identified and therefore were not taken into consideration.

This is quite understandable. My thesis is that the forces which encouraged the rise of Chinese policies were *primarily government policies* facing the Overseas Chinese and economic development strategies which were *never intended* to promote the rise of the Chinese. That they have done so is *primarily an unintended effect*. In retrospect, Indonesia and the Philippines adopted a *de facto* industrial policy for the Overseas Chinese.[9]

The first part of this *de facto* industrial policy is to persuade the intended beneficiaries to abandon their present economic activities which though presently profitable would soon be in decline. The Indonesian government *de facto* forced such abandonment.

In March 1955 the Indonesian government announced that the ownership of rice mills was limited to indigenous Indonesians. Nonindigeneous owners (i.e. the Chinese) were required to transfer ownership to indigenous citizens within a two-year period.

In March 1957 fifteen industries, mostly in light manufacturing were reserved for operation by Indonesian citizens only. Businesses owned by alien Chinese in the proscribed fields were to be transferred to Indonesian citizens.

In January 1960 the ministry of trade implemented a government decision stating that aliens would no longer be allowed to engage in retailing in the rural areas below the agency level.

The above policies therefore invalidated the premise of Williams that the Chinese businessmen would have *no* incentive to leave their presently lucrative business.[10] Having forced the majority of Chinese businessmen to divest themselves of their existing businesses and so generate investible funds, the Indonesian government then implemented the second component of the *de facto* industrial policy, providing attractive investment opportunities. Again, the official and intended objective was to implement an economic development plan for Indonesia.

Like most economic development plans, *Repelita* (the Indonesia economic development plan), while recognizing the role of agriculture in economic development, was premised on industrialization as the basis for economic development. Moreover, such industrialization was to be attained through import-substitution. The government policies which were adopted to encourage import-substitution consisted of government support in terms of high tariff rates, access to government credit, and market monopoly and government guarantees in terms of protection from expropriation, exemption from some government regulations, and lower tax rates.[11]

The Indonesian industrialization strategy provided the major impetus for the rise of the Chinese industrialists for several reasons:

1. The government decision to intervene in the working of the marketplace created distortions in terms of price differentials and supply disruption and provided new opportunities for corruption in terms of licenses and government credits and subsidies.[12] In effect, the number of possible business deals that could be generated multiplied geometrically, thus providing a competitive advantage for the Chinese trading companies. (One perverse indication of this competitive advantage is the alleged ability of Chinese businessmen to offer bigger bribes. Economists explain this phenomenon in terms of greater efficiency rather than looser morality on the part of the Chinese businessmen.) From such deals and from the divestment of their existing businesses, the Chinese were able to generate the investible funds which Williams felt could not be raised by the Chinese community.

2. The economic plan indicated the industries where the Chinese businessmen could place their investible funds. Moreover, the economic plan was integrated into the lending program of the the state-owned banks, thus assuring additional long-term capital for the Chinese investible funds. One foreign economist in Jakarta estimated that over a five-year period from 1969 to 1974, two-thirds of all commercial bank credit was made available to *non-pribumi* (namely, Chinese) businesses.[13]

3. The government policies (tariff protection, low interest rates, market monopolies) assured the profitability of such investments.[14] This is what is meant by *institutionalizing the business deal*. Where before the Chinese entrepreneur could only rely on the uncertain market place to consummate his business deals successfully, he now had the institutional support of the government in assuring the success of his business deals. This institutionalization of the business deal eliminates the element of uncertainty and freezes the market imperfections upon which the business deal is usually based.

4. The government guarantees, not only in terms of assured profitability but also in terms of exemption from nationalization or expropriation, provided the incentive for the Chinese businessmen to make the long-term commitments which the transition from trading to manufacturing required. The government *de facto* provided assurance against expropriation for investments in pioneer industries which were more credible than may have ordinarily been possible by providing a mechanism for veiling Indonesian Chinese investment. Since foreign investors were welcome for the pioneer industries, the Indonesian Chinese businessmen could recycle their funds as investment coming from foreign investors.[15] An idea of the magnitude of possible

investments by Indonesian Chinese using Singaporean, Hong-kong and Taiwan fronts is presented in the Table V-1; and

Table V-1
Stock of Foreign Investments in Indonesia
Selected Southeast Asian Countries
1976

Country of Origin	Stock of Foreign Investment (US $ 000)
Hong Kong	728,300
Philippines	272,100
Singapore	115,600
Taiwan	106,000
Malaysia	42,700
Total 1,264,700	

Sources: U.N. Centre on Transnational Corporations, *Transnational Corporations in World Development*, page 247 and Louis T. Wells, Jr.,*Third World Multinationals: The Rise of Foreign Investment from Developing Countries*, pp. 164 and 172.

5. The government policies minimized the need for a change in the business and management structure of the Chinese businesses. The effect of government policies which assured profitability for participants in the industrialization program was to convert managerial expertise into a *desirable rather than necessary* component of economic performance. In other words, a company protected by tariff walls, subsidized by low-cost debt and awarded a market monopoly does not need managerial competence to be profitable. Moreover, government policies on allowing foreign investors to enter into joint ventures with Indonesian business groups also provided access to technical and managerial expertise to the Chinese industrialists. Conversely foreign investors found the Chinese firms to be the most attractive of joint venture partners. For example, in its June 1-7, 1974 issue, *The Economist,* in an article entitled, "The Chinese are Multinational," stated that every Japanese joint venture in Singapore and Malaysia is in partnership with the Chinese and that 90 per cent of Japanese investments in Indonesia and Thailand have been made through Chinese middlemen. This is understandable The Overseas Chinese businessmen provided business expertise, an already existing distribution network, and a buffer for whatever illicit activities (primarily corruption) which operating in a developing country may entail but which carries stiff penalties for violation in the home country of the foreign investor (primarily the United States). Incidentally, this is one area of operations in developing countries where family corporations hold a distinct corporate advantage over Western multinationals and state-owned enterprises.[16]

In summary, the prediction of Williams that Chinese business-men would *not* evolve into industrialists turned out to be incorrect. However this was due *not to faulty reasoning but to incorrect premises*. Thus he could not foresee that:

1. The Chinese would be given an incentive to abandon their present trading business and enter into new manufacturing businesses.
2. The Chinese would gain access to sources of capital and management.
3. The Chinese, in certain designated industries would be able to draw upon government support.

This point is most aptly illustrated in the rise of the two most prominent Chinese industrialists in Indonesia: Liem Sioe Liong and William Soeryadjaya.

Liem Sioe Liong started his business career in Indonesia as a twenty year old Fukien-born immigrant in the Central Java town of Kudus in 1936.[17] After serving for about ten years as an apprentice in his uncle's peanut-trading business, Liem branched out on his own in *kretek* (clove) trading. He bought the *kretek* from the farmers and then sold the product to clove cigarette producers (trader strategy).

During this period, Liem also developed the personal connections that would serve him in good stead in his future business career. In the struggle for independence against the Dutch (1945-1949), Liem actively supplied the newly established Diponegoro division of the Indonesian army in Central Java with food, clothing, medicine, and military supplies. It was through this support of the fledgling army that he established his links with the future generals of Indonesia, most prominent of whom was General Suharto.

In the 1950's, aware of the policies of the Indonesian government on Chinese traders in the local areas, Liem went into manufacturing (textiles, nails, and bicycle parts) and moved his base of operation to Jakarta. His move to transform his business was effectively carried out. However, his growth and expansion were constrained by the policies of then President Sukarno.

By 1966, with the collapse of the Sukarno government and the rise to power of Suharto, Liem suddenly acquired all the necessary components to undertake business deals. The most prominent and most successful of these deals was the clove concession. In 1968 Liem's PT Mega, together with another company, was granted the exclusive right to import cloves (entrepreneur strategy level). While Indonesia was a producer of cloves, large domestic consumption was required importats. And Indonesia's clove imports are substantial (US$ 120 million in 1981).

The clove import license, while lucrative as a business deal, could not be institutionalized in the sense that PT Mega would have assurance that this right would continuously be awarded to the company. The establishment of Bogasari Flour Mills provided the mechanism for institutionalizing the business deals which Liem was able to generate. The flour mills (with installed annual capacity of 1,800,000 tons of wheat flour and 600,000 tons of bran in 1983) operated by Bogasari provided assurance that the awarding of flour monopoly rights to Bogasari could be justified on economic grounds and would be difficult to transfer to another business group. Moreover, Bogasari further strenghtened its claim on the monopoly by establishing a grey-cotton weaving unit to produce flour bags and a bulk-shipping unit (eight bulk carriers of 220,000 DWT in 1983) to transport wheat from the United States, Canada and Australia to Indonesia.

Using the Bogasari deal as a model, the Liem group has diversified into cement manufacturing (Indocement) . Indocement has nine fully operational lines with an aggregate capacity of 9.5 million tons per year. With this capacity, Indocement has become the largest cement producer in Southeast Asia, and Cibinong, where all its operational lines are concentrated, is probably the largest single cement complex in the world.

The Liem Group's institutionalization of a business deal is also amply demonstrated in the Krakatau Steel-Cold Rolling Mill Indonesia Utama deal.[18] Krakatau Steel is a state-owned Indonesian enterprise which owns the country's single integrated steel complex in Cilegon, West Java, 120 miles West of Jakarta. The steel complex includes a direct reduction plant with a total capacity of two million tons, a billet plant with a 500,000 tons-a-year capacity, a bar mill, a sections mill, a wire-rod mill, a slab mill with a 1.1 million tons-a-year capacity and a hot strip mill with a 1-million tons-a-year capacity. Krakatau has however been an unprofitable operation. To turn Krakatau around, the Indonesian government, despite its preference for *pribumi* (native or indigeneous) entrepreneurs, called on the Liem Group. Interestingly, the solution proposed by the Liem Group was *not* based on streamlining operations but on formulating a deal whose profits would offset the losses from the operations of the steel plant. Basically the deal involves the Liem Group though its trading expertise, assuring the disposal of Krakatau Steel's production at full capacity (where previous capacity utilization was only 50 per cent) through the establishment of a cold rolling mill (Cold Rolling Mills Indonesia Utama), through the imposition of tariffs and through exclusive importation and exportation rights granted to PT Giwang Selogam. Figure V-2 presents the deal in greater detail.

While the Liem group sought to institutionalize its business deals through government support or partnership, the Soeryadjaya sought to institutionalize its business deals through partnership with Japanese multinationals.

FIGURE U-2
THE KRAKATAU-CRMI BUSINESS DEAL

PROBLEM: Krakatau Steel operating at 50 per cent of capacity and at an estimated annual loss of US$ 45 million. Morever, even if capacity utilization were raised to 100 per cent of capacity, Krakatau steel would still be *unprofitable*.

SOLUTION IN FOUR STEPS

COMMENTS

STEP 1:

Krakatau Steel and Liem Group organize Cold Rolling Mills Indonesia Utama (CRMI). CRMI would process hot-strip coils from Krakatau Steel into cold-rolled coils. Total Project Cost to be funded as follows:

Commercial Loans	US$ 240 million	30 %
Export Credit	320 million	40 %
Equity	240 million	30 %
Total	800 million	100 %

Krakatau creates demand for hot-strip coils, thus allowing Krakatau Steel to operate at full capacity. Liem Group with US$ 96 million controls US$ 800 million project.

Equity Structure would be as follows:

Remaining problems:

Krakatau Steel	US$ 96 million	40 %
Ciputra	48 million	20 %
Liem Group	96 million	40 %
Total	240 million	100 %

Krakatau's lower but still continuing *unprofitability*. Expected *unprofitability* of CRMI.

Step 2

Indonesian government imposes import restrictions on products produced by Krakatau and CRMI: steel billets, wire rods, hot-strip coils, sheets and plates and cold-rolled coils. Critics claim such action raises domestic prices by an average of 10 per cent.

Prices for output of CRMI and Krakatau steel can now be raised by 10 per cent and still be competitive.

Step 3

PT Giwang Selogam designated sole importer for certain steel products (1982 value about US$400 million). For cold-rolled steel PT Giwang Selogam quotes US$550 a ton in contrast to US$430 a ton if imported directly.

Through PT Giwang Selogam and through CRMI, Liem Group now controls supply for cold-rolled coils in Indonesia. Profits can now be used to help Krakatau Steel.

Step 4

PT Giwang Selogam commits to buy Krakatau Steel's excess production at high domestic price of US$350 a ton and export it at a loss. Also,

Liem Group neutralizes criticism against PT Giwang Selogam, helps Krakatau all net earnings of PT Giwang Selogam after deducting losses on exports of hot-strip coils will be remitted to Krakatau Steel to reduce its losses.

Steel to attain profitability while assuring profitability of CRMI. *Cost of subsidy to Indonesian not visible though real nevertheless.*[19]

Starting his business career as trader of scrap newspaper in Cirebon at the age of nineteen in 1942, William Soeryadjaya eventually saved enough capital to finance an education (a two-year tannery course in Holland), an attempt at small-scale manufacturing, and lastly an import-export firm.[20] After almost a decade of slow growth (also during the Sukarno presidency), P. T. Astra, the trading company of Soeryadjaya completed a business deal which clinched the future of the company.

Awarded a contract in 1967 to supply power generators to the Indonesian government, P. T. Astra opened a US$2.8 million letter of credit in favor of General Motors, the proposed supplier of the power generators. The Agency for International Development (AID) of the United States which was funding the Indonesian government for this specific projected contested the award. Stymied by legal difficulties, Soeryadjaya decided to buy instead 800 Chevrolet trucks from the same company. Between the opening of the letter of credit and the placing of the truck order, the rupiah plummeted from Rp 141 to Rp 317 against the U.S. dollar, giving the company an exchange gain alone of 124 per cent. Moreover, the new government of Suharto had undertaken a massive rehabilitation programme for roads and irrigation systems. There was therefore a need for heavy trucks and only P. T. Astra could supply them off the shelf.

With the capital accumulated from the business deal and with the knowledge of the bright prospects of the transport industry in Indonesia, William Soeryadjaya sought to institutionalize his business deal. Taking over and refurbishing an automotive assembly plant owned by an unsuccessful state enterprise (Gaya Motors), Soeryadjaya was able to negotiate a joint venture with Toyota of Japan.

The linkage with Toyota provided P.T. Astra with access not only to the technical expertise and financial resources of Toyota but also with a model for institutionalizing the business deal for P.T. Astra. Building on this joint venture experience, P.T. Astra negotiated similar agreements with other multinational companies; Honda for motorbikes, Daihatsu for commercial vehicles, Peugeot and Renault for passenger cars, Komatsu for tractors, and Fuji-Xerox for office copiers. By 1982, the P.T. Astra group consisted of 60 companies, 21,000 employees and a turnover that exceeded US$1.7 billion. Table V-2 presents the major components of Soeryadjaya's business group.

Table V-2
Astra Subsidiaries and Affiliates

Company	Percentage Astra Ownership
Astra Graphia	100.00 %
Midas Oil	100.00
Astra Motor Sales	85.00
Federal Motor	85.00
Daihatsu Indonesia	70.00
United Tractors	55.30
Multi Astra	54.25
Gaya Motor	51.83
Skylift Indonesia	42.45
Toyota Astra Motor	41.40
Toyota Mobilindo	40.00
Maxiferro Steel	37.50
Honda Federal	34.00
Town and Country Properties	28.55
Hazemeyer Holec Indonesia	25.00
Nippondenso Indonesia	22.50
Kayaba Indonesia	20.00
KGD Indonesia	17.00
Wardley Summa Leasing	10.00

Source: *Asian Finance*, December 15, 1982, page 102.

In comparison to the Liem group, the Soeryadjaya group, with its closer link to multinational companies, had been more willing to bring in professional managers. (It must be stressed however, that like the Liem group, its competitive advantage lies not so much in its management capability but more in its joint venture arrangements.) In 1972, the company hired a Dutch executive to establish an accounting system (the Western double-entry as compared to the Chinese cash-flow system) which earned the certification of a reputable accounting firm. Since 1981, the company, not surprisingly, has adopted management techniques from Japan such as quality circles.

As will be discussed in chapter six, the management structure and operations remain uniquely Chinese. In its profile of the company, the magazine, Asian Finance (December 15, 1982) contrasted Astra International with Sime Darby:

> Astra's claims to prominence are borne out by a comparison of its financial profile with, for example, that of Sime Darby, justly reputed to be ASEAN's largest corporate enterprise.

> Although in terms of total assets, Astra's US$560 million is just about half of Sime Darby's US$1.2 billion, its turnover of a little above US$1 billion is only a wee bit behind the US$1.14 billion Sime Darby posted at the end of June 1982. And this year, Astra expects its turnover to exceed US$1.5 billion.

> There is a vital difference nevertheless. Astra is a closely-held family enterprise in the traditional mould of Chinese immigrants, unlike Sime Darby, which has a multinational spread of equity.[21]

In the Philippines, the government followed essentially the same *de facto* industrial policy with respect to the Chinese. The Philippine government first enacted laws to force the Chinese businessmen out of trading and agriculture.[22] Then, pursuing an industrialization policy based on import-substitution, the government in effect directed the flow of the recently liquified Chinese investments into protected industries.

In May 1954, the Philippine Congress passed Republic Act No. 1180, generally known as the Retail Trade Nationalization Law. Signed into law by President Magsaysay, the law required all alien-owned stores to close within a period of ten years. The net effect was a decline of Chinese-operated stores from 16,245 in 1945 to 13,000 by 1960.[23]

In May 1960, Republic Act No. 3018 stipulated that all alien-operated business in the retail and wholesale trade, cultivation, and transportation were to cease operations in two years (mills and warehouses within three years). The law was effectively implemented. The number of alien-owned firms in the rice and corn industry in the Philippines declined from 6,109 at the time of the enactment of the law to 2,177 within two years. By the end of 1962, the number had dwindled further to 400 and had all but disappeared by 1964[24].

The question that naturally arises from such effective implementation of the law is where the Chinese capital was tranferred. Yuan-li Wu and Chun-hsi Wu, in their book, *Economic Development in Southeast Asia The Chinese Dimension*, argue that Chinese capital transferred from retailing to wholesaling, foreign trade, and manufacturing. There are several indications that support this argument.

For one, indicators of the mix of Chinese investment show an increasing percentage invested in manufacturing (Table V-3).

Table V-3
Indicators of Changing Mix of Chinese Investment in the Philippines

Sector	1948[a]	1955[b]	1963[b]	1979[c]
Commerce	75.8%	63.0%	57.0%	52.3%
Industry	18.4	29.2	31.0	42.7
Others	5.8	7.8	12.0	5.0
Total	100.0	100.0	100.0	100.0

Sources: Yuan-li Wu and Chun-hsi Wu, *Economic Development in Southeast Asia: The Chinese Dimension*, pages 75 and 78 and G. L. Hicks and S. G. Redding, "Culture and Corporate Performance in the Philippines: The Chinese Puzzle," in *Essays in Development Economics in Honor of Harry T. Oshima*, Table 1.
[a] Based on estimates of Chinese investment.
[b] Based on Chinese investment in newly registered business organizations. Indicator may therefor overstate actual Chinese investment in manufacturing.
[c] Based on the sales of Chinese firms in the Top 259 Philippine corporations in 1979.

Another indicator of the movement of Chinese investment into manufacturing is the increase in the number of Chinese firms among the top manufacturing companies. In a 1968 study[25,] 66 out of the top 254 (26.0 per cent) manufactuing companies were Chinese-owned. In a 1979 study,[26] 47 out of the top 140 (33.6 per cent) manufacturing companies were Chinese-owned.

In transfering from trading to manufacturing, the Chinese business was transformed from a disfavored investor into a protected investor. In an article entitled, "Effective Rates of Protection in the Philippines," Norma Tan provides empirical proof of the protection afforded by government policy:

Table V-4
Effective Protection Rates in the Philippines
1974

Industry Group	Effective Protection Rate
Agriculture and primary	4.6 %
Manufacturing	43.0
Exports	9.1
Import-competing*	26.0
Import-noncompeting*	50.2
Overall	33.3

Source: Norma Tan, "Effective Rates of Protection in the Philippines, 1974," in *Journal of Philippine Development*, Number Ten, Volume V, No. 2, 1978, pages 185-212.
* By definition, more than 10.0 per cent of total domestic supply is imported.
* By definition, less than 10.0 per cent of total domestic supply is imported.

B.Coping with the Political Environment: Malaysia

In the cases of Indonesia and the Philippines, the rise of Chinese industrialists was permitted by the governments concerned as the price for the implementation of the country's economic development program. In Malaysia, this trade-off was neither politically feasible nor even economically necessary.

When Singapore left the Federation of Malaysia in 1965, what was achieved was not only a political solution to the racial issues raised by the presence of Singapore in the federation. In addition, Malaysia was freed from the need to support an industrial base (Singapore) and could therefore concentrate on improving its agricultural base. In his book entitled,*The Economies of the ASEAN Countries: Indonesia, Malaysia, Philippines, Singapore and Thailand*, Brian Wawn pointed out the results of such an economic development strategy:

At the time of independence in 1957, tin and rubber dominated the economy, accounting for one third of employment and two thirds of exports. Malaysia has since diversified successfully, establishing other important primary products and a fast growing manufacturing sector. There are now six major export categories, each forming 9–25 per cent of total exports in 1980. These are, in order: crude oil, manufactures; rubber; logs and sawn lumber; palm oil and tin. Growth in manufactures has been based on labor intensive products, notably electronic components, textiles, clothing and wood products.

Given such an economic development strategy, the opportunity for institutionalizing business deals never arose for the Malaysian Chinese businessmen. The Malaysian government passed no laws forcing the divestment of Chinese investments in specific areas, thus providing no motivation for liquifying Chinese investment in mature industries. Moreover, the decision not to actively pursue industrialization provided no new areas of investment of Chinese capital into government-protected and government-supported pioneer industries.

Even if such an opportunity existed, it is unlikely that the Malaysian Chinese would have been allowed to exploit it, given the political climate then prevailing in Malaysia. Moreover, unlike the Philippines and Indonesia, the Malaysian government inherited from the departing British a highly trained administrative bureaucracy.[27] Mobilized by the racial riots which erupted in Malaysia in 1969, the Malaysian government focused its energies on solving what it perceived to be the root cause of such conflict: the substantial inequality in income among the races.

In 1971, the Government of Malaysia formally adopted into its five-year economic development plans the New Economic Policy (NEP). The NEP sought to restructure Malaysian society so as to achieve by 1990 a community where all the racial groups consisting of the Malays, the Chinese and the Indians will participate as full partners in the socio-economic development of the nation.

After several attempts at promoting the development of *Bumiputra* (Malay) entrepreneurs, the Malaysian government adopted a bold strategy of leapfrogging to Managerial Capitalism, bypassing Entrepreneurial Capitalism.[28] To attempt solely a strategy of developing Malay entrepreneurs (assuming this were possible on a sufficient scale) would merely freeze the economic gap between the races. To accelerate the economic development of the Malay sector, the Malaysian government took control of professionally managed British companies such as Sime Darby and Guthrie Corporation and sought to transfer both ownership and management to the Malays. The chosen instrument for such a transfer was *Permodalan Nasional Berhad* (National Equity Corporation).

The objective of PNB was clear. As Table V-5, shows, PNB has the major responsibility for increasing the share in the ownership and control of the corporate sector of the *Bumiputra* from 12.4 per cent in

1980 to 30.0 per cent in 1990. The task is made more difficult by the assumption that the corporate sector of Malaysia will keep growing at a healthy pace.

Table V-5
Ownership and Control of the Corporate Sector
1971-1990

Year	Bumiputra[a]		Other Malaysians[b]		Foreigners[c]		Total	
	M $000	%	M $000	%	M $000	%	M $000	%
1971	279.6	4.3	2,233.2	34.0	4,051.3	61.7	6,564.1	100.0
1975	1,394.0	9.2	5,653.2	37.5	8,037.2	53.3	15,084.4	100.0
1980	3,273.7	12.4	10,544.1	40.1	12,505.2	52.5	25,323.0	100.0
1990[d]	16,800.0	30.0	22,400.0	40.1	16,800.0	30.0	56,000.0	100.0

Source: *Fourth Malaysia Plan, 1981-1985*, page 68
[a] Refers to the Malays (54 per cent of the population) as well as to agencies like PNB who hold shares in trust for the Malays.
[b] Refers to the Malaysian Chinese (35 per cent of the population) and to the Malaysian Indians (11 per cent of the population).
[c] Refers primarily to the British and the Singaporeans.
[d] Our calculations based on a growth rate of 8 per cent per annum and based on a target share of 30 per cent for the Bumiputras and the other Malaysians maintaining their 1980 share of 40 per cent.

The strategy which PNB adopted to attain its objective contained the following major components:
1. In terms of funding, PNB obtained interest-free loans from the *Bumiputra* Investment Foundation (which had previously received funding from the Malaysian government). By 1983, the total outstanding loan was M$3.7 billion (M$3.2 billion non-interest bearing and M$0.5 billion interest bearing).
2. In terms of acquiring shares in the corporate sector, PNB had two major sources of corporate shares:
    a)   The shares in private companies owned by several government institutions such as *Perbandanan Nasional* (National Corporation of Malaysia which was more widely known as PERNAS). PNB was able to buy substantial portions of these agencies' investment portfolios at a good price. For example, following the transfer of some of its major assets to PNB, the current assets of PERNAS fell by a third and its operating profit was halved from M$1.13 billion to M$594.4 million. At the net level, a profit of M$ 66.8 the previous year was turned into a loss of M$102.9 million after taking into account a massive extraordinary loss of M$122 million arising from the sale of shares to PNB.
    b) The publicly listed shares of foreign companies operating in Malaysia. On September 1981, PNB conducted a "dawn raid" on Guthrie Corporation shares which were traded on the

London Stock Exchange. While this sudden move drove up the price of Guthrie from 662p per share to 901p per share, control of Guthrie Corporation, the second largest corporation in Malaysia after SIME DARBY (a British corporation acquired by PERNAS in 1976) was lost by British management in three hours. Six weeks later, the Malaysia operations of Harrison and Crosfields, the third largest company in Malaysia were also acquired.

3) In terms of transferring the acquired shares in the corporate sector to individual *Bumiputras*, PNB organized a mutual fund called *Sekim Amanah Saham Nasional* (SASN) managed by a PNB company called *Amanah Saham Nasional Berhad* (ASNB). Shares in the mutual fund, SASN were then sold by the management company, ASNB to qualified Bumiputras on easy installment terms. The Bumiputra investor merely had to invest 10 per cent of the price of the mutual fund shares and the PNB would guarantee that the dividends from the mutual fund would be at least enough to pay off the 90 per cent balance in nine years.

Faced with such a sophisticated strategy being implemented by an effective administrative machinery and funded adequately by government revenues, the Malaysian Chinese had to formulate their own strategy, choose an alternative administrative machinery, and tap their own resources.

Unlike the Indonesian Chinese, the Malaysian Chinese had more numerous sources of long-term capital. For one, the Singapore banks like the Oversea Chinese Banking Corporation (OCBC) and the United Oversea Bank (UOB) had retained the Malaysian branches which were established when Malaysia and Singapore were part of British Malaya. They, of course could be expected to give preference to Chinese borrowers. Secondly, both Malaysia and Singapore had very active stock exchanges which traded the shares of Malaysian and Singaporean companies. Malaysian Chinese businessmen could draw on these exchanges for their capital requirements through rights and new stocks offerings.

Most importantly, the Chinese in Malaysia, unlike most Chinese in Southeast Asia have participated actively, albeit on a minority basis, in Malaysian politics. The organization through which they have primarily channeled their political actitivities is the Malaysian Chinese Association. Since its founding in 1963, Malaysia has been governed by a coalition called *Barisan Nasional* (National Front). The coalition consists of three major political parties representing the three races – the United Malays' National Organization (UMNO); the Malaysian Chinese Association (MCA) and the Malaysian Indian Congress. (It is interesting to note that the MCA was based on the Chinese Chambers of Commerce[29] while the MIC was based on the Indian-led labor unions[30].) Unlike the Chinese in Indonesia and the Philippines, the Malaysian Chinese wielded *direct* political power.

The objectives of the Malaysian Chinese could be stated as follows.

1) At the very least, to maintain their 40 per cent share of the corporate sector. To do so, and still allow the *Bumiputras* to increase their share would mean that the increased share of the *Bumiputras* would come at the expense of foreigners rather than the Chinese.

2) As Malaysian citizens, to be given the opportunity to bid and take over several of the foreign companies.

3) As the dominant business group, to transform the successful family corporations into modern organizations capable of providing competition to the professionally managed companies (i.e. SIME DARBY) being taken over by the *Bumiputras*.

The strategy selected by the Malaysian Chinese was to create parallel business organizations which possess as their competitive advantage direct and evident political power and *not* just access to political power as in the case of Indonesia and the Philippines. A prime example of such parallel business organization is Multi-Purpose Holdings. (Interestingly, the selected strategy of the Malaysian Indians was to copy the Chinese strategy and form their own holding company called Maika Holdings.)

Multi-Purpose Holdings provides an illustration of the major components of the selected strategy of the Malaysian Chinese seeking to establish themselves as industrialists.[31]

1) A tangible if informal linkage with a political organization.

2) A diversified source of funding.

3) A share in the take over of foreign companies.

4) An attempt at professionalization of the management.

The linkage between Multi-Purpose Holdings (MPH) and the Malaysian Chinese Association is evident and compelling. The timing of its birth identified its parentage. The company was incorporated in August of 1975 as part of the Chinese reaction to the controversial Industrial Coordination Act (ICA) introduced in April 1975 (four months before the creation of MPH). The Act was considered onerous by the Chinese in terms of its coverage of businesses which had to comply with *bumiputra* participation (a form of affirmative action or quota). Chinese businesses employing as few as twenty five people and having a minimum capital of M$100,000 were affected by the Act.

The response of the Chinese through the Malaysian Chinese Association was twofold. On the political front, amendments were proposed in Parliament to soften the Act. Such changes were enacted in 1977 and 1979. On the economic front, the response was the formation of MPH.[32]

The equity structure of MPH reflects its MCA linkage. The initial capital of MPH was subscribed to largely by individual MCA members at the urging of the party (officially, MPH is open to all the races). When the first public issue of MPH was made, the biggest institutional investor was *Koperasi Serbaguna Malaysia* (Multi-Purpose Cooperative Society of Malaysia). KSM was formed nine years earlier by the youth wing of the Malaysian Chinese Association. Later, KSM organized a mutual fund similar to that organized by PNB specifically to invest in MPH. Called the Multi-Purpose Investment Fund, the fund acted as limited form of unit trust allowing KSM to transfer ownership of MPH directly to its members.

By 1983, Multi-Purpose had a total of 450 million shares with an estimated market value of M$1.2 billion. Table V-6 presents the ownership structure of MPH as of September 1982.

Table V-6
Equity Structure of Multi-Purpose Holdings
September 1982

Stockholder	Group Number	Holdings Percentage
KSM-Multi-Purpose Fund	234.0 million	52.0 %
Malaysian Chinese Individuals 32,000 shareholders)	199.0 million	44.2
Nominee Companies	15.5 million	3.4
Non-Chinese Malaysian Individuals	1.5 million	0.4
Total	**450.0 million**	**100.0 %**

Source: Jeffrey Segal, "A bamboo umbrella," *Far Eastern Economic Review*, September 3, 1982, pp. 93-96.

While the bulk of its equity financing was Malaysian Chinese based, MPH sought to diversity its sources.[33] Apart from listing its share in the Singapore Stock Exchange, MPH was able to place some its shares in London. A London brokerage firm, James Capel, placed about six million shares with its London clients (mainly institutional investors).

MPH has also relied heavily on banks for several syndicated loans. Its 1982 Annual Report lists an international cast of bankers ranging from the multinational banks (Chase Manhattan and Chartered Bank) to ASEAN banks (Oversea Chinese Banking Corporation) to Malaysian banks (Malayan Banking Berhad) to a captive bank (United Malayan Banking Corporation).

In summary then, the strategy of creating a mass base of individual investors, the institutional support of a political organization, the facade of international ownership and the financial support of a multitude of reputable banks, while perfectly justifiable on purely business grounds, also defines perfectly a strategy shaped significantly by the political environment.

Based on this strategy, the acquisitions could be explained in terms of the Malaysian Chinese claiming their share of the British firms being taken over by Malaysians, claiming their share of Malaysia's basic resources such as prime urban land and agricultural plantations, protecting and promoting the interests of Malaysian Chinese firms, and diversifying as a hedge against an uncertain political future.

An example of MPH claiming its share of the British firms was the acquisition of the trading subsidiary of Guthrie Corporation (PNB, as stated previously took over the rest) and of the plantations of Dunlop Holdings and of Plantation Holdings. Bandar Raya, on the other hand was acquired for its real estate holdings. An unusual acquisition has been Magnum which with its gambling operations (a lottery linked to the results of the local horse races) protects it from competition from the *Muslim Bumiputras* (its main competition is the Genting Highlands Casino, a Chinese-owned operation).

The political clout of MPH has its limitations. In 1982, MPH, bought the shares in United Malayan Banking Corporation of Chang Ming Thien who died in March of that year. The objectives of MPH were to retain the shares under Chinese ownership and to establish a bank for the group. However, the result of the acquisition (50.22 per cent ownership of the bank) displaced the state trading corporation, PERNAS, as the biggest stockholder. The political outcry that ensued forced MPH to reduce its holdings to the same level as PERNAS (40.68 per cent) and to settle for equal representation on the bank board.

If MPH was frustrated in its attempt to build a bank-based business group similar to the Japanese *zaibatzus* or Korean *chabols*, it has neverthess proceeded to build a Japanese-style international trading house (*sogo shosha*). The trading arm acquired from Guthrie was renamed Multi-Purpose International Trading Corporation (MITC). MITC with its branch network in Southeast Asia was beefed up with shipping and light manufacturing operations. Figure V-3 presents the group structure of Multi-Purpose Holdings as of April 1983.

The example of Multi-Purpose has been emulated by other Chinese groups and by the state organizations of the Malaysian Chinese Association. The Hainanese, Hakka and Hokkien dialect associations have established their own trading company. The Associated Chinese Chambers of Commerce and Industry have a holding company called Unico. More importantly, various state MCA organizations have follwed suit. Table V-7 presents the MCA state organizations with their respective holding companies.

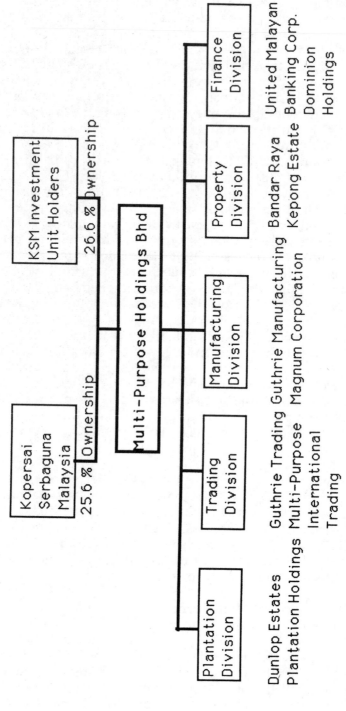

FIGURE V-3

MULTI-PURPOSE HOLDINGS ORGANIZATIONAL CHART

Kopersai Serbaguna Malaysia

25.6 % Ownership

KSM Investment Unit Holders

26.6 % Ownership

Multi-Purpose Holdings Bhd

Plantation Division

Trading Division

Manufacturing Division

Property Division

Finance Division

Dunlop Estates Plantation Holdings

Guthrie Trading Multi-Purpose International Trading

Guthrie Manufacturing Magnum Corporation

Bandar Raya Kepong Estate

United Malayan Banking Corp. Dominion Holdings

Source: Multipurpose Holdings Berhad 1982 Annual Report, Far Eastern Economic Review,   May 10, 1984

Table V-7
Holding Companies of MCA State Organizations
September 1982

State	Holding Company	Paid-Up Capital
Perak	Peak Hua Holdings	M$ 20 million
Johor	Matang Holdings	10 million
Selangor	Aik Hua Holdings	20 million
Pahang	Pan Wa Holdings	20 million

Source: Jeffrey Segal, "A bamboo umbrella," *Far Eastern Economic Review*, September 3, 1982, pp. 93-96.

C.Building on the Resource Base: Thailand

Like Malaysia, the economic development strategists of the government of Thailand opted to build on the agricultural base of Thailand rather than pursue vigorously an industrialization strategy.[34] This decision is rooted in the long tradition of agricultural production as the mainstay of the economy. (As early as the 1920's Thailand had been exporting rice to British Malaya.) As a consequence, the percentage of rural population to the total population is 85 per cent compared with 65 per cent for the Philippines. For another, the percentage of agricultural exports to total exports is 55 per cent compared to 35 per cent for the Philippines. Despite this difference in development strategy and the resulting difference in the economic profile, Thailand and the Philippines have roughly the same per capita GNP. Moreover, the Thais could point to one significant advantage of its agriculture-based development strategy; the percentage of households in the Philippines with income below US$300 is 41 per cent while that for Thai households is 22 per cent.

If the decision of the economic planners of Thailand to concentrate on agriculture provided no opportunities for the type and size of business deals which became prevalent in Indonesia and the Philippines, neither were the Chinese in Thailand forced to divert their entrepreneurial resources to comply with an uncertain political environment as the Malaysian Chinese were forced to do. While Thailand, like its ASEAN neighbors, had enacted laws restricting the business operations of Chinese businesses, Thailand was less zealous in their implementation. Moreover, in 1973, Thailand *switched* its Overseas Chinese policy from one of restriction and control to that of assimilation.[35]

The turnaround in policy can be traced to the recommendations of a special commission established in 1971 for the purpose of studying and submitting recommendations on the so-called Chinese problem. In its 1973 report the commission basically recommended that:

1) It would be impractical to try and replace the Chinese through competition in the market or to seize national economic control by political means.

2) It would be more practical to initiate cooperation with the Chinese in seeking to develop the Thai economy.

3) It would not be adviseable to reserve certain areas of the economy for Thai nationals alone as the indigeneous Thais must be encouraged to develop the Chinese characteristics of industriousness, a work ethic and a keen awareness of the rigorous demands of economic life and the free market.

Given these differences in economic development strategies as well as in national policies with respect to the Overseas Chinese, it may be tempting to ask if the predictions offered by Williams would now prevail. In fact, they did not. That they did not can be attributed to Bangkok Bank[36], the largest commercial bank in the ASEAN countries, as well as to other Thai Chinese bankers[37] which became catalysts in encouraging and financing Chinese entrepreneurs to become Chinese industrialists (more accurately, agro-industrialists).

Although Thailand was never colonized by the Western powers, commercial banking in Thailand was dominated by the Western banks prior to the Second World War. In fact the first commercial bank in Thailand was established by the British in 1888. The first Thai bank was founded in 1906, eighteen years after the first foreign banks. During World War II, the Thai government, influenced by the Japanese, closed all the foreign banks (except the Japanese bank). This provided the opportunity for the opening of Thai-owned banks.

Prior to this opportunity, Thai merchants who were mostly Chinese were confronted with great difficulties in their dealings with the foreign banks. To assist them in such dealings, they usually availed themselves of the services of Thai businessmen who had both access and credibility with such banks. Such men were called *compradors*.

One such *comprador* was a Thai businessman named Chin Sophonpanich, an ethnic Chinese who was born in Thailand and educated in China. Together with several investors, Sophonpanich established Bangkok Bank in November of 1944 with a paid-up capital of Baht 1 million[38], a deposit base of Baht 9 million and a staff of 23 people.

The initial client base of Bangkok was the Thai-Chinese businessmen in the trading sector. The credit structure of the bank in 1950, where over half of the credits were in the form of discount and rediscount bills, reflected that focus.

Moreover, in 1954 Bangkok Bank gained a distinct competitive advantage in serving this lucrative market by opening a branch in Hong Kong (even before opening another metropolitan branch and twenty years ahead of any locally incorporated bank in Thailand). In addition to developing trade between Thailand and Hong Kong, the opening of the Hong Kong branch enabled the bank to tap the considerable financial resources of the Overseas Chinese deposited in the safe haven of Hong Kong, as well as to open a linkage with the international banks based in Hong Kong.

Building on this competitive advantage over the local banks, Bangkok Bank expanded rapidly to Tokyo (December 1955), to Singapore (March 1957), to London (June 1957), to Kuala Lumpur (January 1959), to Saigon (1962), to Taipei (May 1965), and to Jakarta (1969). By 1976, the bank's fifteen (15) overseas branches and offices (out of a total of 191 bank branches) contributed 41.6 per cent of total bank profits.

By 1975, Bangkok Bank handled 45 per cent of the country's export and 33 per cent of its import trade finance. A breakdown of its loans and advances attested to its trade-oriented focus.

Table V-8
Loan Portfolio Mix of Bangkok Bank
June 1975

Sector	Percentage Share
Wholesale and Retail Trade	39 %
Import-Export	19
Manufacturing	18
Construction and Real Estate	6
Agriculture	1
Mining	1
Others	16
Total	100 %

Source: *Banker*, November 1975, pages 1404-1407.

By 1983, Bangkok Bank was the largest bank in Southeast Asia with total assets of Baht 160 billion (about US$8.0 billion), 293 branches and more than 18,000 employees. In Thailand, Bangkok Bank accounted for about a third of the country's institutional credit and stood far above the local competition (its asset base is about 2.5 times its closest competitor, the state-run Krung Thai Bank). Bangkok Bank has, however, remained a trade-oriented financing institution.

The success of Bangkok Bank has been financially rewarding for the Sophonpanich family. In 1983, Institutional Investor magazine

Table V-9
Domestic Loan Portfolio Mix of Bangkok Bank
April 1983

Sector	Percentage Share
Trading Companies	45%
Industry	23
Agriculture and Mining	8
Services and Others	24
Total	**100 %**

Source: *Far Eastern Economic Review*, July 28,1983, pp. 52-59.

placed Chin Sophonpanich as among the world's top twelve richest bankers whose fortunes exceed US$1 billion each. A survey[39] of the fortunes of the 36 wealthiest families (mostly of Overseas Chinese origin) in Thailand conducted by a Bangkok-based American researcher put the Sophonpanich family at the top of the list with holdings in 154 companies. From such a base, Chin Sophonpanich has established links with the Liem Group of Indonesia, the Hong Kong-based group of Robert Kwok and Robin Loh, as well as the Harapan and Frank Tao groups.

One of the Thai-Chinese companies which benefitted from the developmental work of Bangkok Bank as a bank client is Charoen Pokphand[40], the biggest agro-industry firm in Southeast Asia.

Started in 1921 by two brothers, Chia Ek Chaw and Chia Seow Whooy who emigrated to Thailand from Swatow, China; Charoen Pokphand grew from their initial business of trading in vegetables in Bangkok's Chinatown. In 1954, the two brothers decided to go into feedmilling and established Charoen Pokphand Feedmill Co. (Charoen Pokphand is loosely translated as"progress in agricultural products").

After discovering a growing market for animal feeds, the company decided to integrate its operation by raising poultry. Despite their awareness of the existence and the size of the market, CP's efforts at tapping such a market were only modestly successful. They attributed this to problems with the poultry stock and breeding.

Thus, the breakthrough for the company occurred in 1970 when it was able to negotiate a joint venture agreement with Arbor Acres Farm Inc. of the United States. Given the access to agricultural technology, the company experienced tremendous growth and diversification in the agribusiness industry and in the ASEAN region.

By 1985, the CP group of companies (60 in Thailand and 20 overseas) was engaged in a wide range of agribusiness activities that involved ferilizers, agrochemicals, pesticides and herbicides, tractors, animal feed, livestock operations in poultry and swine, crop farming, and processing of farm produce; and in allied manufacturing; jute-backed carpets, polypropylene, and packaging. Its joint-venture partners from the United States in addition to Arbor Acres (poultry) were DeKalb (corn, seed, and swine production), PIC (pig stock), and Continental Grain (feed mills).

In Asia, CP has operations in Indonesia (five feedmills), Malaysia (a chicken-raising project), Singapore (a feedmill and swine-raising project), Taiwan (two feed mills), Hong Kong (one feedmill) and the People's Republic of China. In Singapore, for example, CP has a joint venture with the Singapore government in a swine-raising project involving the production of 250,000 head of swine per year.

From its operational base in Thailand CP operates the biggest feedmill operation (six feedmills) and handles nearly half of Thailand's estimated chicken exports of 9,290 tons (1977–78). In addition, CP exports frozen chickens to Singapore, the Middle East, Rumania, and Germany; live pigs to Hong Kong and Singapore; cassava and tapioca to the European Economic Community; corn to Taiwan, Singapore, Hong Kong, Japan, Malaysia and Indonesia; fish meal to a number of Asian countries; and carpets to the European Economic Community and to the United States.

In 1982, the CP group of companies had an estimated sales of US$ 1.0 billion and a worldwide workforce of 12,000. As a private company owned mainly by the Chiaravanont family (Chiaravanont is the Thai name taken by the children of the two founders), CP does not publicly declare its profits. It does, however, still in the Chinese tradition assert that " the group depends on a high volume of transactions with small margins."

D.Alternative Intermediation Strategies: Singapore

In 1965, Singapore, then a state in the Federation of Malaysia, was asked to withdraw from the federation. This unprecedented act of a nation to actively divest itself of a vital part of its territory and its citizenry were motivated solely by political considerations. The other states of Malaysia and the native Malays were concerned that with Singapore in the union, political power would be added to the considerable economic power of the Malaysian Chinese.

The consequences of the expulsion were far-reaching. For one, the creation of the independent state of Singapore established the first country in Southeast Asia to be politically controlled by the Overseas Chinese. For another, Singapore's initial economic development strategy, which was similar to those of Indonesia and the Philippines, had to be completely revised. The separation from Malaysia meant the subsequent loss of an agricultural sector (Malaysia) to finance the import requirements of an industrial sector

(Singapore) and the loss of a captive market (Malaysian consumers) to subsidize the higher priced and lower quality output of the infant industries (Singaporean factories).[41]

The revised economic development strategy of Singapore could then be divided into two major components: the creation of a manufacturing sector with the capacity to compete internationally and the institutionalization of Singapore as the entreport and the distribution center of the Southeast Asian countries in general and of ASEAN in particular. In a sense, Singapore sought to do for the ASEAN economic community what every Chinese distributor sought to do within each of the ASEAN countries.

Indicators of Singapore's intermediation function abound. For example, in 1960 90 per cent of Singapore's export was classified as entreport export: exports for which Singapore acts merely as the transhipment center. In 1981 Singapore had the distinction of having the world's third largest refining center after Rotterdam and Houston. Table V-10 presents statistics suggesting the magnitude and range of the role played by Singapore as a distribution center for the ASEAN countries.

Table V-10
Singapore as Distribution Center for ASEAN

	Indonesia	Malaysia	Philippines	Singapore	Thailand
Land Area (sq. ms.)	735,000	128,000	166,000	230	198,000
Population (1977)	136.9 m	12.6 m	44.7 m	2.3 m	44.2 m
Oil Refining* (000 bpd,1981)	400	150	200	1,060	175
Merchant Fleet[b] (000 grt, 1975)	859	226	879	3,892	183
Air Transport[c] (million, 1975)	1,600	1,000	1,600	3,200	1,600
Asia-Dollars (assets of ACU[d])	nil	nil	nil	US$ 54 billion	nil

Sources: Brian Wawn, *The Economies of the ASEAN Countries: Indonesia, Malaysia, Philippines, Singapore and Thailand*, and Thomas Allen, *The ASEAN Report*.
* Expressed in barrels per day (bpd)
[b] Expressed in gross registered tons (grt)
[c] Expressed in passenger-miles (p-m)
[d] Asian Currency Units (ACU) are financial institutions specifically organized to accept deposits and deal in U. S. dollars.

One of the competitive strengths which Singapore brings to bear on its economic development strategy of being the business center of the ASEAN countries is its commercial banking system.[42] The three largest private commercial banks in Singapore - the United Overseas Bank (UOB), the Oversea Chinese Banking Corporation (OCBC), and the Overseas Union Bank (OUB) - grew out of a strategy of serving the Chinese business community not only in Singapore but also in the ASEAN countries. (For example, the separation of Singapore from the Federation of Malaysia did not result in the closure of the OCBC branches in Malaysia.) Moreover this strategy had been followed as early as the 1900s.[43]

Commercial banking in Singapore officially started in 1840 when three British exchange banks - Mercantile Bank, the Hongkong and Shanghai Bank and the Chartered Bank — opened branches in Singapore. These banks, as well as the ensuing American and Dutch banks, concentrated primarily on financing the import and export of the foreign businesses such as the British plantations. The growing market of Chinese businessmen was not served except indirectly through the financing of the foreign firms which in turn extended financing to their Chinese *compradores* (middlemen). In addition to the language problems, the Chinese businessmen were not conversant with the formalities of Western banking such as the signing of documents and the placing of collateral. The Western banks, on the other hand, were not flexible enough to eschew collateral-based lending and to lend on the basis of business reputation and good faith. In 1903, the first local Chinese bank, called the Kwong Yik Bank, was founded. The bank, organized by the Cantonese community, catered primarily to that sub-market. Other Chinese communities such as the Teochews and the Hokkiens followed suit.

The Oversea Chinese Banking Corporation was the result of the merger in 1932 of three Chinese banks founded by Hokkien merchant groups: the Chinese Commercial Bank, the Ho Hong Bank and the Oversea Chinese Bank. The corporate strategy which the bank has pursued since its founding was shaped by the circumstances of it formation and the business philosophy of Tan Chin Tuan.

The merger of the three Chinese banks in 1932 was dictated primarily by their weakened position. The Great Depression of the 1930s had severe repercussions for the economy of British Malaya (present-day Malaysia and Singapore) in general and for the banks in particular. For example, total exports of Malaysia fell from $ 1,290 million in 1925 to $366 million in 1932, while imports fell correspondingly from $ 1,008 million in 1925 to $380 million in 1932. The price of rubber fell from $1.14 per pound in 1925 to $0.07 per pound in 1932.[43] (This would be equivalent to a decline in the price of oil from $32.00 per barrel to $1.96 per barrel.) Given this background, it is not surprising that the objective of OCBC is to be "solid as a rock" and that its operating creed has been "Safety First at all times."

The man who faithfully and effectively implemented such a strategy was Tan Chin Tuan. Starting his business career in 1925 as a clerk in one of the merged banks, Tan Chin Tuan served as managing director for forty years and by 1982 had served as Chairman for sixteen years. The major bank policies which Tan Chin Tuan followed were conservative asset management and lending policies, a conservative board of directors, and a long-term investment outlook.

The board of directors of OCBC were drawn from the ranks of successful and established businessmen. By themselves, they controlled or commanded business resources equal to or even exceeding the bank's total deposit base. As such, the bank was under no pressure either to lend to them or to pursue an aggressive strategy.

Given its conservative outlook, the bank under Tan Chin Tuan, who had a legendary reputation for picking winners, concentrated on building an investment portfolio of blue-chip securities and prime real estate properties. Moreover, such investments were not restricted to Singapore alone.

Lim Mah Hui, who wrote a paper on the ownership of the top 100 corporations of Malaysia in 1974, identified OCBC as representing the most significant participation of Chinese capital (Singaporean and Malaysian) among the top 100 Malaysian corporations. OCBC is estimated to have an interest in 38 out of the 100 top corporations with significant holdings in 13 out of the 100 corporations. OCBC's ownership include Fraser and Neave (31.6 per cent), Malayan Breweries (44.4 per cent), Straits Trading (36.1 per cent) and United Engineers Limited (22.0 per cent). Lim Mah Hui had this to say about OCBC:

> The OCBC group in Malaysia and Singapore is what the house of Morgan or Rockefeller is to the United States. It is the largest and oldest local bank in Malaysia and Singapore with combined assets in 1976 of $4.3 billion and net worth of $929 million. Its activities span the fields of banking, insurance, tin mining and smelting, plantations, trading, hotel, properties, investments, manufacturing, and management services.
>
> The group is owned and controlled primarily by a few Singaporean and Straits Chinese families. The ownership and control interests have remained rather stable in its entire history...
>
> OCBC is thus a Chinese family dominated bank, with most of the families keeping a low profile, tending their own family businesses and allowing a few selected directors, namely Tan Chin Tuan, Yong Pung How and S. Q. Wong, who is a major shareholder and is associated with the Great Eastern Life Assurance, to play a public role representing their interests.
>
> The importance of OCBC in the Chinese business community is revealed in its history. Almost all Chinese businessmen of great repute have at one time or another passed through its portals.[44]

If OCBC represented the traditional vehicle (banking and investment) of intermediation in the ASEAN countries by the Singaporean

Chinese companies, then Promet Bhd represented a new form of intermediation; a partnership between a Malaysian Malay and a Singaporean Chinese to create ASEAN's first significant international oil and construction company.[45]

That a Malaysian Malay would consider a Singaporean Chinese a preferable partner to a Malaysian Chinese is justifiable on several grounds. For one, the Singapore Chinese, not being a citizen of Malaysia, would have no option to build a political base. This would then stabilize the basic relationship in the partnership where the Malaysian partner contributes his political skills while the Singaporean partner contributes his business skills. For another, in terms of business skills, the Singaporean Chinese in relation to the Malaysian Chinese provides greater access to the international economy in general and to the other ASEAN countries in particular. Lastly, such an arrangement would have less appeal to the Malaysian Chinese who have built their own political base and could argue for retaining their 40 per cent in all Malaysian companies. The Singaporean Chinese as foreigners would always be under pressure to divest in the future.

Promet Bhd. started its business life in 1971 as a Singaporean company called Promet Pte. Ltd. Promet operated principally as a trading and servicing company catering to the offshore oil industry by providing procurement and offshore maintenance services. The contacts in the offshore-oil industries were developed by its founder, Brian Chang, in his previous capacities. Born in South Africa and having graduated from London University in 1965, Chang assumed a succession of jobs in Asia with Mobil Oil, Vosper Thornycroft and Far.East Asia Shipbuiding. In forming Promet, Brian Chang envisioned the creation of a marine-based engineering company. Coming into operation at the height of the oil exploration boom in Southeast Asia, the company prospered.

In its first year of operation, Promet generated a turnover of S$3 million and a profit of S$150 thousand. In 1973, Chang sold 40 per cent of Promet to Jardine Matheson of Hongkong. Boosted by this tie-up with the Hongkong multinational, Promet was able to put up a 24-hectare fabrication yard on the west coast of Singapore. By 1980, the company had grown to be one of the four major rig-builders in Singapore and had diversified into the construction of jetties, dredges, barges and other items of advanced marine equipment.

In 1980, Brian Chang launched a complex takeover of Bovis Southeast Asia, a losing Malaysian affiliate of a British-based construction company. The main assets of Bovis were its Malaysian registration and its listing at the Kuala Lumpur Stock Exchange. In the restructured company, which became Promet Berhad, Brian Chang was joined by a classmate of London University days, Tan Sri Ibraham Mohamed. The transformation of Promet into a Malaysian corporation and the entry of Tan Sri Ibrahim Mohamed with a 30 per cent stake offered several significant advantages:

1) The 30 per cent stake of Tan Sri Ibrahim Mohamed (lodged in the family holding company, Fawanis Sdn. Bhd.) satisfied Malaysia's local-participation requirements under the New Economic Policy.

2) Tan Sri Ibrahim Mohamed's close relationship with Dr. Mahathir Mohamed, who became Prime Minister of Malaysia in 1981, provided political support and access to the upper echelons of the government of Malaysia.

3) As partial payment for its 30 per cent stake in Promet, Fawanis transferred a 24-hectare plot of land in south Johore and the Aurora Beach Hotel in Bintulu, Sarawak. These properties provided the initial base for the company's property development projects.

One of the first property deals to be finalized in Malaysia was the acquisition of the Belmont Centre in Kuala Lumpur. Renamed Promet Centre, the project was completed at a cost of M$90 million and expected to generate a peak rental income of M$50 million annually. By December of 1981, plans were finalized for the construction of a M$250 million fabrication yard for marine structures and equipment to be located at Telok Rumunia in Southeast Johore. By 1983 Promet was able to announce the start of two billion-dollar projects. Pulau Langkawi (an island south of Penang) was to be converted into a tourist's paradise at a cost of M$4 billion (M$2.34 to US$1.00). Another recreational centre was to be constructed at Trengganu for a total cost of M$1.0 billion.

The transformation of Promet Pte. Ltd. of Singapore into Promet Sdn. Bhd. of Malaysia can best be illustrated by the changing sources of its profits from 1982 to 1984.

Table V-11
Sources of Promet Pre-tax Profits

Source	1982	1983	1984
Singapore marine fabrication	64 %	27 %	16 %
Malaysian property development	-	46	53
Malaysian construction	11	6	8
Malaysian fabrication	-	5	7
Granite, quarrying and transportation	25	16	16
Total	100 %	100 %	100 %

Source: *Far Eastern Economic Review*, March 31, 1983, p. 68.

E. *The Williams Hypothesis Demonstrated: Brunei*

There is one ASEAN country where the premises for the prediction of Williams were valid. In Brunei, the following premises of Williams were operational[46]:

1. The Chinese businessmen in Brunei who dominate the private sector were under no pressure to move out of their existing businesses;
2. The Brunei government, awash in oil revenue and blest with a small population of 200,000 people, did not have to formulate any aggressive economic development strategy which would provide incentives and guarantees for the Chinese to move into industry;
3. The economic and political environment of Brunei did not encourage the rise of financial institutions which would have been the catalysts for any movement by Chinese businessmen into industry.

The Chinese businessmen in Brunei, like their Chinese counterparts in Southeast Asia, also dominate the private sector of their country of residence. But *unlike* their Chinese counterparts in Southeast Asia, their dominance of the private sector causes *no resentment* from the native population and so *no interference* (and conversely *no unofficial patronage*) from the Brunei government. Thus the Chinese who constitute about thirty per cent of the population[47] own most of the shops and the service industries as well as a significant presence in construction and the companies servicing the oil and gas industry.

The reason for such indifference to the Chinese dominance in the private sector can be explained by one word: **oil.**

Brunei is in the same situation as Saudi Arabia, a country ruled by a monarch (Sultan Sir Muda Hassanal Bolkiah), sparsely populated by a people professing the Muslim faith, and sitting on a vast reservoir of oil. In 1983, Brunei produced 175,000 barrels of oil per day and exported all but 10,000 b/d. In addition, Brunei in 1982 ranked fourth in world production of natural gas, exporting all of its production of 12.6 million cu. ms. of LNG to Japan. In 1982 these oil and natural gas exports earned for Brunei more than B$8 billion (about US$4 billion).

The bulk of the export earnings go the Brunei government. For fiscal year 1983, state revenues were B$6.1 billion while state expenditures were only B$1.7. Thus, even after appropriating B$600 million into a development plan, the state, in the words of its British-educated financial minister, had "a fair margin of surplus." In addition to this current surplus, the Brunei government has an investment portfolio of about US$ 3.5 billion from which it can draw should the need ever arise.

While the state expenditures are modest relative to state revenues, in absolute terms they provide its citizens with substantial benefits. For one, the government employs 70 per cent of the estimated indigenous work force of of 45,000 (there are 25,000 foreign workers). For another, citizens of Brunei enjoy free education and health care, subsidized loans for cars and housing, subsidized rice (90 per cent imported from Thailand) and beef (shipped from a Brunei-owned cattle ranch in Australia), subsidized pilgrimages to Mecca and even subsidized funeral expenses. Lastly, there are no income taxes for individuals.

Such generosity on the part of the goverment does not even put any pressure on the foreign exchange reserve of the government. While everything except oil is imported, 1982 merchandise imports totalled only B$1.7 billion and so resulted in a trade surplus of B$6.6 billion.

Under such an environment it is difficult for Chinese industrialists to develop. Firstly, eighty per cent of the gross domestic product comes from energy, leaving only about twenty per cent for activities where the Chinese can operate. Table V-12 presents a more detailed breakdown of the contribution of activities to the gross domestic product.

Table V-12
Contribution to Gross Domestic Product by Economic Activity
Brunei

Economic Activity	1979
1. Agriculture, Forestry and Fishing	0.7 %
2. Mining and Manufacturing*	81.4
4. Wholesale and Retail Trade	8.8
5. Construction, Transport and Communication	2.5
6. Banking, Finance and Insurance	0.6
7. Services and Others	6.0
Total	100.0 %

Source: *Brunei State Chamber of Commerce Jubilee Journal, 1980-1981*, p. 26.
* almost completely oil and natural gas production.

Secondly, the Chinese businessmen have no resource base to build upon. Since all agricultural requirements are imported, there is no agriculture to speak of. (The Agricultural Department, with an annual budget of B$16 million, employs about 2,000 people but there are fewer than 100 farmers).

Thirdly, ninety per cent of the Chinese are non-citizens. Prior to independence, the Brunei Chinese, as residents in a British Protectorate, carried British-Brunei passports. With independence, Brunei Chinese who are non-citizens were merely issued certificates of identity. Since it is difficult to obtain citizenship, Chinese businessmen could not own land (and hence, real estate development projects) and could not set up financial institutions (hence, no catalyst).

Under these conditions, the Chinese of Brunei have fulfilled the prediction of Williams and have not risen to become industrialists.

F.*Summary*

This chapter has sought to provide a range of case studies on the interplay between the private profit-maximizing operations of the Overseas Chinese firms and the public economic development policies of the ASEAN government in the shaping of the corporate strategies of the Chinese Industrialists. The developing-country environment of the ASEAN countries as well as the common economic position and social system of the Overseas Chinese shaped the development of the common generic strategies of the Chinese trader, distributor and entrepreneur. The diverse economic development plans of the ASEAN countries stimulated diverse strategies among the Overseas Chinese industrialists in each of the ASEAN countries. Indonesia and the Philippines, sharing a common industrial development strategy, spawned the common strategy of the Chinese industrialists in these countries, a strategy based on institutionalizing business deals arising from government policies. In Malaysia, where the government instituted a New Economic Policy aimed at removing income inequality on a racial basis, the Chinese industrialists developed a business strategy based on political support and protected their share of the economic pie. In Thailand the government policy of agricultural development and assimilation of the Overseas Chinese allowed the Chinese businessmen of Thailand to pursue corporate strategies based on two resource bases; the agricultural economy and the Chinese business community of Thailand. Singapore sought to expand its entrepot role in ASEAN into the financial center for the ASEAN countries. In pursuit of this objective, Singaporean bankers have performed the traditional intermediation role while Singaporean businessmen have developed innovative mechanisms for forging business partnerships with other ASEAN businessmen. Lastly, in Brunei the conditions which Williams thought would prevail in Indonesia, actually prevailed: a class of Chinese merchants profitably engaged in trading and a government with no incentive to draw on the entrepreneurial skills of the Chinese. As predicted by Williams, Brunei did not see the rise of the Chinese industrialists.

NOTES

1. Lea E. Williams, "Chinese Entrepreneurs in Indonesia," *Explorations in Entrepreneurial History*, October 1952 First Series, Volume 5, Number 1, pp. 34-60.
2. For purposes of this book, we define those Chinese businessmen engaged in the production of goods as *industrialists* and consider all Chinese businessmen above the level of traders as entrepreneurs.
3. Williams, p. 59.
4. Anthony Rowley, "Birth of a multinational," *Far East Economic Review*, April 7, 1983, pp. 44- 56.

5. Indonesian Chinese have been advised by the Indonesian government to adopt Indonesian names. So most Indonesian Chinese have a Chinese name and an Indonesian name.
6. David Jenkins, "Giving credit where it is due," *Far Eastern Economic Review*, September 21, 1979, pp. 113-116.
7. Williams, p. 49.
8. Max Weber, The *Religion of China* (Glencoe, Illinois: The Free Press, 1951), p. 104.
9. The good news for proponents of industrial policy is that it works. The bad news is that for industrial policy to work, the stated intention of the industrial policy must to discriminate a*gainst* the intended beneficiaries.
10. Yuan-li Wu and Chun-hsi Wu, *Economic Development in Southeast Asia: The Chinese Dimension* (Stanford: Hoover Institution Press, 1980), pp. 173-174.
11. For a brief description of economic development policies of the ASEAN countries, see Brian Wawn, *The Economies of the ASEAN Countries: Indonesia, Malaysia, Philippines, Singapore and Thailand* (New York: St. Martin's Press, 1982)
12. For examples of government corruption due to intervention in the market place, see Louis T. Wells, Jr., "Bribery and Extortion inInternational Business, Case # 9-380-087, *Harvard Business School,* 1979
13. David Jenkins, "Giving credit where it is due," *Far Eastern Economic Review*, September 21, 1979, p. 113.
14. G. Y. Adicondro, "From Chinatown to Nan Yang: An Introduction toChinese Entrepreneurship in Indonesia," *PRISMA*, No. 13, 1979, pp. 67-85 for examples of such policies.
15. Based on an interview with a Singaporean banker whose bank acted as trustee for the investment of Indonesian Chinese into Indonesia. In effect, the Indonesian government is officially informed that the Bank is in fact the investor when it is merely acting as trustee. For the more wary Indonesian Chinese, the bank would form a Singaporean company which could also act as the official investor, with the real identity of the investor hidden under two layers; the Singapore company and the Singapore bank. Given such secrecy, it is therefore impossible to estimate what percentage of investments in the name of Singaporean or Hong Kong nationals is actually owned beneficially by the Indonesian Chinese.
16. Louis T. Wells, Jr., The *Third World Multinationals: The Rise of Foreign Investment from Developing Countries* (The Massachusetts Institute of Technology Press, 1983), p. 141.
17. Manggi Habir and Anthony Rowley, "The extended (corporate) family of Liem Sioe Liong," *Far Eastern Economic Review*, April 7, 1983, pp. 51-56;"Liem Group's overseas thrust takes shape," *Asian Finance*, December 15, 1982, p. 101; and T. K. Seshadi, "Salim's billion dollar empire," *Asian Finance*, May 15, 1980, pp. 29-30.
18. Susumu Awanohara, "Krakatau's production is coated in confidentiality," *Far Eastern Economic Review*, June 23, 1983, pp. 60-62 and Manggi Habir, "Murky downstream," *Far Eastern Economic Review*, April 26, 1984, pp. 188-189.
19. Estimates of the social cost and benefits of such a project would be difficult. While it is easy to calculate the additional cost to the economy in terms of higher steel costs, about $112 million per year, the benefits of an integrated steel mill are more difficult to quantify.
20. Amitabha Chowdhury, "Corporate Leader of the Year: William takes Astra back to grassroots," *Asian Finance*, November 15, 1983, pp. 104-122 and "Astra's financial muscle paves way for expansion," *Asian Finance*, December 15, 1982, pp. 102-103.
21. "Astra's financial muscle paves way for expansion," *Asian Finance*, December 15, 1982, pp. 102-103.
22. Yuan-li Wu and Chun-hsi Wu, *Economic Development in Southeast Asia: The Chinese Dimension* (Stanford: Hoover Institution Press, 1980), pp. 73-80.
23. Ibid., pp. 177-178.
24. Ibid., p. 77.
25. Kunio Yoshihara, "A Study of Philippine Manufacturing Corporations," in Shinichi Ichimura, *Southeast Asia: Nature, Society and Development* (Honolulu: The University Press of Hawaii, 1976), pp. 244-268.
26. G. L. Hicks and S. G. Redding, "Culture and Corporate Performance in the Philippines:The Chinese Puzzle," in *Essays in Development Economics in Honor of Harry T. Oshima* (Manila: Philippine Institute for Development Studies, 1982).

27. For a description of the British-trained Malayan civil service, see Khasnor Johan, *The Emergence of the Modern Malay Administrative Elite* (Singapore: Oxford University Press, 1984). For a critique of the Philippine bureaucracy, see Walden Bello et al., *Development Debacle: The World Bank in the Philippines* (San Francisco: Institute for Food and Development Policy, 1982). For a critique of the Indonesian bureaucracy, see Awaloedin Djamin, "The Administration of Public Enterprise in Indonesia," Unpublished DPA Thesis, *University of Southern California*, 1963.

28. Limlingan, "The Coming of Managerial Capitalism in Malaysia," Unpublished mimeograph, 1985.

29. Margaret Roff, "The Malayan Chinese Association, 1948-65," *Journal of Southeast Asian History*, Vol. 2, 1965, pp. 49-53.

30. See Michael Stenson, *Class, Race and Colonialism in West Malaysia: The Indian Case* (Sydney: University of Queensland Press,1980).

31. Jeffrey Segal, "A bamboo umbrella, "*Far Eastern Economic Review*, September 3, 1982, pp. 93-96.

32. Anthony Rowley, "The politics of business," *Far Eastern Economic Review*, May 10, 1984, pp. 83-88.

33. Rowley, "An enterprise of many and conflicting purposes," *Far Eastern Economic Review*, May 10, 1984, pp. 88-90.

34. Limlingan, "The Visible Hand in Southeast Asia," Unpublished mimeograph, 1985.

35. Yuan-li Wu and Chun-hsi Wu, *Economic Development in Southeast Asia: The Chinese Dimension* (Stanford: Hoover Institution Press, 1980), p. 72.

36. "Bangkok Bank," *Banker*, November 1975, pp. 1404-1407; "The Bangkok Bank over the years," *Bangkok Bank Monthly Review*, February 1982, pp. 47-63; Paisal Sricharatchanya, "A matter of might and men," *Far Eastern Economic Review*, July 28, 1983, pp. 52-59; Barun Roy, "A redesigned Bangkok Bank gets ready for its future," *Asian Finance*, December 15, 1983, pp. 44-47; "Thailand's new-style bankers," *Business Review (Thailand)*, February 1984, pp. 19-27; and "Continued expansion at Bangkok Bank,"*The Banker*, August 1984, pp. 53-54.

37. A similar though less successful Thai Chinese banking family is the Lamsam family. See "Thai Farmers Bank," *Business in Thailand*, April 1980, pp. 50-61. What is unusual about the bank is the market (the Thai farmer); the strategy (diversification from trading); the continuing succession of Lamsam family members to the presidency (Choti Lamsam to Kasem Lamsam to Bancha Lamsam and to Banyong Lamsam) and the simultaneous program to professionalize the management.

38. At that time Thailand was under Japanese influence. Under its Pact of Alliance with Japan, Thailand maintained its official exchange rate for the Thai baht on parity with the Japanese. So Baht 1 million is equivalent to about Yen 1 million or about US $5,000. See *Bank of Thailand, Economic and Financial Report, 1944*, p. 15.

39. Peter E. Beal, "The Empire Builders, Part I," *Investor (Thailand)*, February 1981, pp. 9-10.

40. Ho Kwon Ping and Kamolwan Sonsomsook, "The little chicken farm is laying golden eggs," *Far Eastern Economic Review*, July 11, 1980, p. 57; Peter E. Beal, "The Empire Builders, Part II, " *Investor (Thailand)*, March 1981, p. 10; Richard Borsuk, "Thailand's Agricultural Multinational Sprouted From Family-Run Seed Shop," *The Asian Wall Street Journal Weekly*, August 1, 1983, p. 4; and Ruth Karen, "Charoen Pokphand: Pig Raising in Four Experimental Villages in Thailand," in Simon Williams and Ruth Karen, *Agribusiness and the Small-scale Farmer: A Dynamic Partnership for Development* (Boulder, Colorado: Westview Press,1985), pp. 111-124.

41. Limlingan, "The Visible Hand in Southeast Asia." Unpublished mimeograph, 1985.

42. Dick Wilson et al., *Solid As A Rock: The First Forty Years of Oversea Chinese Banking Corporation* (Singapore: OCBC Limited, 1972); Dick Wilson, "Oversea Chinese Banking Corporation," *Banker*, December 1975, pp. 1468-1470; Quek Peck Lim, "Exploring the intricacies of Tan Chin Tuan's OCBC," *Euromoney*, July 1979, pp. 96-106; Padraic Fallon, "The Tide in the Life of Tan Chin Tuan," *Euromoney*, October 1982, pp. 140- 152; and Patrick Smith and Frieda Koh, "Roots in a migrant past," *Far Eastern Economic Review*, August 20, 1982, pp. 59-59.

43. Dick Wilson et al., *Solid As A Rock: The First Forty Years of Oversea Chinese Banking Corporation* pp. 3-5.
44. See Lim Mah Hui, "The Ownership and Control of Large Corporations in Malaysia: The Role of Chinese Businessmen," in Lim and Gosling, *The Chinese in Southeast Asia: Identity, Culture and Politics* pp. 285-289.
45. Patrick Smith, "Fall and rise of a chameleon," *Far Eastern Economic Review*, March 31, 1983, pp. 63-68 and Ranjit Gill, A perfect pair," *Insight*, January 1984, pp. 6-17.
46. See Rodney Tasker, "Nervously into the world," *Far Eastern Economic Review*, March 12, 1982, pp. 22-28 and V. G. Kulkarni, "Young, rich and eligible," *Far Eastern Economic Review*, January 26, 1984, pp. 28-34.
47. The 30 per cent figure for the Chinese share of the total population, was based on V. G. Kulkarni, "Young, rich, and eligible," *Far Eastern Economic Review*, January 26, 1984, p. 29. The 1974 estimate of Yuan-li Wu and Chun-hsi Wu cited in Table I-2 was much higher at 47 per cent. We would attribute the discrepancy to problems of definition of the permanent population (i.e. Chinese workers from Hong Kong having being counted as part of the permanent population by one estimate and not by another); to outward migration of Chinese, and to acquisition of Brunei citizenship by Chinese residents.

CHAPTER VI
THE CHINESE MANAGERIAL SYSTEM

A. *Chinese Culture and the Chinese Managerial System*

In 1980, S. G. Redding of the University of Hong Kong wrote a paper entitled, "Cognition as an Aspect of Culture and its Relation to Management Processes: An Exploratory View of the Chinese Case."[1] In that paper, the author argued that the Chinese firms would not evolve into large-scale enterprises:

> One of the central questions in examining Chinese business practice is whether it is 'emerging'. Many of its characteristics are those of the pre-bureaucracy small business found in Western cultures, and it is assumed by many that the process of development will lead to inevitable adoption of a more rational model capable of sustaining a large enterprise, with all the attendant economies of scale. A growth process was achieved by the Japanese with relatively high speed and with obvious success, but their organizational pattern does not fit the Western bureaucratic model.
>
> In the Chinese case, growth along Western lines, which usually is by growing the corporate body itself, appears to be resisted. There are large Chinese companies, it is true, but they appear still to be run in the same way as small Chinese companies. They remain in family control. Rational/legal authority is not adopted. Size is often achieved by collecting together a set of small businesses and leaving them uncoordinated except at the financial level. More complex forms of large scale enterprises have not developed: **there are no Chinese multinationals** (bold letters mine).[2]

In September of 1983, a Thai business magazine, *Business in Thailand*, featured an article entitled, "The New Multinationals."[3] In that article the business magazine featured the two most significant examples of Thai multinationals, the Charoen Pokphand Group and the Bangkok Bank. Both Thai multinationals, as described in the previous chapter were controlled and managed by Thai Chinese.

As in Chapter five, my objective is not to illustrate the perils of seeking to vindicate one's analysis by its ability to predict the future. Rather, it is to start with a convenient framework for identifying and analyzing the Chinese managerial system.

Redding's confident assertion that the Chinese managerial system would *not* spawn large scale enterprises is based on the following assumptions:

1) The influences of Chinese culture on managerial practices are so significant and so deep as to distinguish and differentiate such

managerial practices from Western managerial practices; in effect, there exists a distinct and identifiable Chinese managerial system.

2) Given such significant differences in managerial systems and given that Chinese firms have demonstrated resistance to adopting the Western managerial system, Chinese firms would be at a *competitive disadvantage* vis-a-vis Western firms outside their protected environment and above a certain size where economies of scale would prevail.

3) Given this disadvantage, *no Chinese firm* can become a multinational as such firms have to operate in several country environments and at a certain level of economy of scale.

My thesis is that while Redding was justified in pinpointing the existence of a distinct and identifiable system, he was not justified in citing the alleged inherent advantage of the Western managerial system to the Chinese managerial system. (As a reflection of this bias, the issue that seems to concern scholars the most is the feasibility of successfully transferring the superior management technology of the West to the developing countries of the East.)[4]

This difference in conclusions can be attributed to the comparative management approach we discussed in chapter one. In essence I cautioned against comparing different managerial systems without considering the strategies that these managerial systems were expected to implement.

As an analogy, I would cite the success of third-world multinationals. Comparative management analysis focuses mainly on comparing the managerial systems of developed as compared to developing countries.[5] Naturally, the conclusion to be expected from such comparisons would be unfavorable to the managerial system of developing countries. And from such conclusions has been derived the prediction of the failure of third world firms attempting to become multinationals. The unstated premise of this prediction is that third-world multinationals would pursue the same strategy as that of the Western multinationals and, given their inferior managerial system relative to the Western model, would not succeed. Not surprisingly, the third-world multinationals did *not* choose to pursue such a doomed strategy.

Seen against the backdrop of such predictions are the documented cases of successful multinationals from developing countries. Louis Wells, in his book *Third World Multinationals: The Rise of Foreign Investment from Developing Countries,*[6] documented the rise and success of such third world multinationals and attributes their success to the strategic fit between the environment they operate in, the marketing strategy they pursue, the structure of operation they adopt, and the managerial system they have developed.

Redding, in the cited article and in many others[7], provides compelling evidence that the managerial practices of Chinese corporations have been significantly shaped by Chinese culture. Redding does more. He provides an conceptual framework for differentiating Chinese culture from Western culture. More importantly, he defines how cultural values are transformed into specific managerial practices.

Basically, Redding begins with a description of Chinese cultural values and norms and proceeds to Chinese paradigms (or ways of thinking and viewing the outside world), to the impact of such paradigms on managerial activities, and to specific managerial practices. Figure VI-1 presents the process in chart form.

Chinese values are deeply rooted in the Confucian philosophy the basic tenets of which are its *focus on the group* rather than on the individual and its *acceptance of authority*. The combination of group focus (collectivism) and submission to authority (*li*) are the foundation for the approved attitudes and behavior patterns, most significant of which are:

1. Submission to authority (parents, elders and superiors) rather than a concern for equality (i.e. Westerners talk of rights, Asians talk of responsibility).
2. Primacy of group harmony (smooth interpersonal relationships) rather than individual preferences and even objective reality (e.g. the Asian hesitance to contradict a superior's statement even if it is patently false).
3. Esteem for the force of example over the validity of ideas.
4. Primacy of broad moral values (i.e. respect for authority) over specialized competence.
5. The strict observance of social rules among different members of society:
   a. between parent and child - respect and gratitude
   b. between brother and brother - respect and harmony
   c. between husband and wife - wifely virtue and husbandly concern
   d. within the clan - mutual support and cordiality.

One of the most significant attribute of such cultural values is the Chinese preoccupation with *face* (the distinction between face [Chinese] and self-esteem [Western] is that self-esteem is the "individual's view of himself,' whereas face is the individual's assessment of how others close to him see him).[8]

Redding cites several surveys of Chinese executives in Hong Kong which testify to the existence and the importance of face. The more general study on the distinguishing characteristics of Chinese values is the study conducted by Hofstede.[9] Hofstede seeks to define the concept of national culture in terms of four dimensions which he

FIGURE VI-1
FROM CHINESE CULTURE TO CHINESE MANAGERIAL SYSTEM

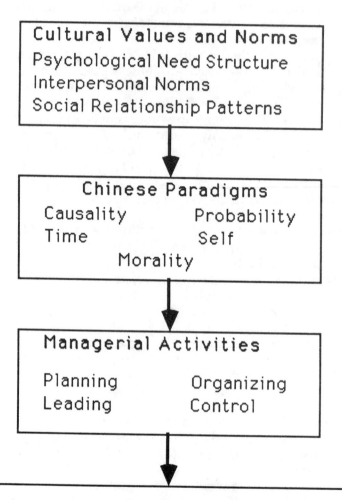

Cultural Values and Norms
Psychological Need Structure
Interpersonal Norms
Social Relationship Patterns

Chinese Paradigms
Causality   Probability
Time   Self
         Morality

Managerial Activities

Planning   Organizing
Leading   Control

Chinese Managerial System

Planning   Policy-making
Control Systems   Organizational Set-up
Leadership Style   Personnel Policies

labels Power Distance, Uncertainty Avoidance, Individualism, and Masculinity-Femininity. Applying the four distinguishing dimensions on forty countries, Hofstede discovers significant variations among different countries.

With respect to Asian countries closely identified with Confucian values (Taiwan, Hong Kong and Singapore), the most significant distinction displayed was, unsurprisingly, in terms of Large Power Distances (a strong hierarchical orientation) and Collectivism (a group focus).[10]

Given these distinguishing cultural values, Redding then cites several studies undertaken by psychologists, anthropologists and other social scientists who argue that people reared in different cultures have different ways of viewing and organizing reality (paradigms).

For example, E. T. Hall in *Beyond Culture* defines two different ways of viewing time: monochronic and polychronic. In a monochronic culture (e.g. American), time is perceived as linear while in a polychronic culture (e.g. Chinese), time is perceived as cyclical.[11]

Redding organizes the different ways of viewing reality into five major areas of cultural differences:

1) Causality - the basic understanding of cause-and-effect relationships between events, activities, and phenomena.
2) Probability - the assessment of probability.
3) Time - the way time is perceived.
4) Self - the view of the individual and his role.
5) Morality - processes of control over human behavior.

Figure VI-2 presents a comparison between Western and Chinese paradigms.

Since Chinese paradigms are fundamentally different from Western paradigms, Redding then suggests that such difference in paradigms have implications for managerial activities. For example, in the case of leadership which is largely the control of people's behavior, Redding argues that people from different cultures have to be led or managed differently.

> If social norms are maintained more by shame than by guilt, then a different set of leadership behaviours may emerge. One might consider two continua, i.e.

The shame continuum

loss of face $\longleftrightarrow$ gain of face

The guilt continuum

failure $\longleftrightarrow$ achievement

Figure UI-2
Western and Chinese Paradigms

	Western	Chinese
Causality	Attempts to understand logical connections between abstracted categories. Use of absolutes. Linear, sequential, explanations	Situational, contextual perception without absolutes. Non-abstract, more sensual perception. Multi-causality
Probability	Future is for calculation. Extrapolation based on logical cause-and-effect.	Fatalism. Calculation seen as naive.
Time	Monochromatic. Scheduling, sequencing, promptness. Coordination possible.	Polychronic. Non-linear. Sense or repetition. Insensitive to timing.
Self	Individual isolated and important in own right. Self actualization. Achievement ethic.	Individual inseparable from social context. Judgment-based relationships. Less pure self-consciousness.
Morality	Guilt. Action to avoid guilt due to infringing absolute moral principles	Shame. Action to avoid due to infringing social norms which are situational.

Source: S.G. Redding, "Management Education for Orientals," unidentified publication.

In the former, control of the individual is external and in the latter internal. Again it is a matter of degree, but Chinese people appear to react to the former than the latter.

Much Western leadership practice is designed to make use of, or sponsor the development of, the need for achievement (e.g. management by objectives, job enrichment, participation, generally holding people to account for a measured individual performance). Such techniques may well trigger off different reactions in a Chinese person and this may be part of the explanation of why such devices are rarely transplanted. The threshold at which face comes into play is very low and difficult for a Westerner to sense and its use as an alternative control device is normal in the Chinese context. In theory, the method of its operations remains problematic.[12]

Hofstede's conclusions agree with Redding's. In the study cited above he argues that U. S. leadership theories are based solely on appealing to the ultimate self-interest of the individual. And so the word "duty," which implies obligations towards others or towards society, does not appear at all in U. S. leadership theories. On the other hand, leadership in a collective society (i.e. Chinese) is a group phenomenon and people are able to bring considerable loyalty to their job, provided that they feel the employer returns loyalty in the form of protection the way a group does.[13]

Using the same analytical approach to the Chinese paradigms in terms of impact on managerial activity, Redding creates the matrix presented in Figure VI-3.

As one of the empirical proofs for the conceptual framework of the Chinese Managerial System which he constructs, Redding refers to a study conducted by Negandhi on the management practices of Taiwanese firms.[14]

The Taiwan study of Negandhi is part of a larger study undertaken in Argentina, Brazil, Chile, Greece, India, Philippines and Uruguay. The approach followed by these studies consists of studying the management practices and effectiveness of U.S. subsidiaries and comparable local firms in each country. This study of management practices includes a firm's orientation toward planning, policy-making, control devices, organizational set-up, the degree of decentralization, leadership style, and manpower management practices. In the Taiwan study, Japanese subsidiaries operating in Taiwan are included for comparison purposes. Figure VI-4 presents the overall profiles of management practices in the U. S. subsidiaries, the Japanese subsidiaries and the Taiwanese firms.

FIGURE VI-3
CHINESE PARADIGMS AND MANAGERIAL ACTIVITY

Chinese Paradigms / Managerial Activity	Causality	Probability	Time	Self	Morality
Planning	Not formally developed	More use of hunch and intuitive; fatalistic view	Low priority to deadlines; non-linearity		
Organizing	Abstract Entities not seperated out		Coordination loose	Personalistic networks	
Leading				High Subjectivity, Obligation nets Paternalism	Sensitivity to face. Pragmatism in business ethics
Control	'Control cycle' not perceived		Problems of urgency and common perception of co-ordinating deadlines.	Objective performance measures not used	Use of shame mechanism.

Source: S.G. Redding, "Cognition as an Aspect of Culture and its Relation to Management Processes: An Exploratory View of the Chinese Case," *Journal of Management Studies*, May 1980, Volume 17, No. 2, p. 143

B. *Comparative Management Analysis and the Chinese Managerial System*

The description of the Chinese Managerial System provided by the Negandhi study uses the Compararative Management Analysis approach. Such approach is quite useful in defining the significant differences between the different managerial systems. However, when the approach moves from the descriptive area (what is) into the evaluative area (which is better), it begins to invite disagreement as to its conclusions. Moreover, when the approach logically moves from the evaluative area (which is better) to the predictive area (what will happen), it opens itself to the possibility of disproof by future events.

The Negandhi study did move from the the descriptive to the evaluative area. Figure V-5 presents the result of the evaluation on

FIGURE VI-4
PROFILES OF MANAGEMENT PRACTICES
U.S. SUBSIDIARY, JAPANESE SUBSIDIARY
AND TAIWAN FIRM

Management Practices	American Subsidiary	Japanese Subsidiary	Taiwan Firm
Planning	Long range (5 to 10 years)	Medium to short range (1 to 2 years)	Medium to short range (1 to 2 years)
Policy-making	Formally stated, utilized as guidelines and control measures	Formally not stated. Not utilized as guidelines and control measures	Formally not stated. Not utilized as guidelines and control measures
Control Devices	Quality control, cost and budgetary control Maintenance. Setting of standards	Quality control Maintenance	Some cost control Some quality control. Some maintenance
Organizational Set-up			
Grouping of activities	On functional area basis	On functional area basis	On functional area basis
Number of departments	5 to 7	5 to 7	5 to 7
Use of specialized staff	Some	None	None
Use of service department	Considerable	Some	Some
Authority definition	Clear	Unclear	Unclear
Degree of Decentralization	High	Low	Low
Leadership			
Style	Consultative	Autocratic	Paternalistic Autocratic
Trust and confidence in subordinates	High	Low	Low
Managers' attitudes toward leadership style and delegation	Would prefer autocratic style. Authority should be held tight at the top	Not available	Would prefer consultative type

*Manpower
Management
Practices*

Manpower policies	Formally stated	Not stated	Not stated
Organization of Personnel Dept.	Not separate unit	Not separate unit	Not separate unit
Job evaluation	Done	Done	Done by very few
Development of selection and promotion criteria	Formally done	Done by some	Done by some
Training programs	Only for the blue-collar employees	Only for the blue-collar employees	Only for the blue-collar employees
Compensation and motivation	Monetary only	Monetary only	Monetary only

Source: Anant R. Negandhi, *Management and Economic Development: The Case of Taiwan,* (The Hague: Martinus Nijhoff, 1973), pages 125-126.

the managerial effectiveness of the American subsidiary, the Japanese subsidiary and the Taiwan firm. Not surprisingly, the American firm was the most effective, followed by the Japanese firm and lastly by the Taiwanese firm.

The Negandhi study concludes by making two points:

1) The utilization of advanced management practices (i.e. American management practices) *does lead* to higher management effectiveness.

2) Based on the results of this study, advanced management practices and know-how are transferrable to the industrial enterprises in Taiwan.

Redding, on the other hand, argues that such advanced management practices are not transferrable to Chinese firms, given the pervasive influence of Chinese culture. Redding then moves from the evaluative to the predictive area by observing that there are no Chinese multinationals, implying therefore that there will be none.

I believe, on the other hand, that the rise of the Chinese multinationals can be explained by the following propositions:

1) That management practices are heavily affected by the corporate culture. In the case of Chinese firms, the corporate culture is, of course the Chinese culture. Thus the question is not which management practice is more effective *per se* but which management practice is most effective for this particular culture.

2) That management practices must fit with the corporate strategies being pursued (i.e. structure follows strategy) and so should *not* be evaluated independently of the strategies.

FIGURE VI-5
PROFILES OF MANAGEMENT EFFECTIVENESS
U.S. SUBSIDIARY, JAPANESE SUBSIDIARY
AND TAIWAN FIRM

Management Effectiveness	American Subsidiary	Japanese Subsidiary	Taiwan Firm
Employee Morale	High	Moderate	Moderate
Absenteeism	Low	Low	Low
Turnover	High	Low	High
Productivity	High	High	High
Ability to attract trained personnel	Able to do so	Somewhat able to do so	Somewhat able to do so
Interdepartmental relationships	Very cooperative	Somewhat cooperative	Somewhat cooperative
Executives' perception of the firm's overall objectives	Systems optimization important goal	Subsystems optimization important goal	Subsystems optimization important goal
Utilization of high-level manpower	Effectively utilized	Moderate to poor utilization	Moderate to poor utilization
Adapting to ronmental changes	Able to adapt without difficulty	Able to adapt with some difficulty	Able to envi-adapt with considerable difficulty
Growth in sales	Phenomenal	Considerable	Considerable to modest

Source: Anant R. Negandhi, *Management and Economic Development The Case of Taiwan*, (The Hague: Martinus Nijhoff, 1973), page 127.

3) That a distinction must be made between family corporations and the Chinese Managerial System. Admittedly, given the personal and even family-type orientation (i.e. William Soeryad-

jaya being called *Oom* [uncle] Willem by Astra employees) of the Chinese managerial system, such a distinction is difficult to bear in mind.

As examples of how management practices depend on corporate culture we would cite group decision-making and lifetime employment. We chose such practices for several reasons. For one these are two managerial practices which the Chinese Managerial System shares with the Japanese Managerial System. For another, these are the managerial practices, which prior to the Japanese economic miracle, were frequently cited as inherent disadvantages of the non-Western managerial systems.

The initial view of group decision-making is that it is time consuming and produces nothing but weak compromises. And the primary example of an ineffective work unit that is usually cited is the committee. However, after studying Japanese decision-making, Peter Drucker reached a different conclusion. In a section entitled "The Effective Decision" in his seminal book, *Management: Tasks, Responsibilities, Practices*,[15] Drucker states:

> The only people who have developed a systematic and standardized approach to decision-making are the Japanese. Their decisions are highly effective. Yet their approach **violates** (bold letters mine) every rule in the books on decision-making. Indeed, according to the books, the Japanese should never be able to arrive at a decision, let alone an effective one.[16]

Drucker argues that the major advantage of the group decision is that once a decision is made, implementation is much easier as the group has been consulted and is therefore committed to implementing the decision. As to the time-consuming effort required to reach a decision, he notes that in the more effective organization, the management is forced to concentrate its time and energy on the big decisions.

Drucker also points out the advantages of lifetime employment. Again the traditional view is that lifetime employment is an inherent disadvantage for managerial systems following such managerial practice. Management scholars who advocate this view argue that lifetime employment is inherently disadvantageous for the following reasons:
1) It generally reduces the incentive to work.
2) It eventually saddles the organziation with incompetent people (the competent having left for greener pasture).
3) It undermines the core authority of management (the right to hire and fire).

Proponents of lifetime employment argue that there are no completely incompetent people; only competent people placed in the wrong positions. And the solution for this error is not to fire people but to move them to the right positions. Moreover, it is argued that lifetime employment forces management to consider what a person can do rather than what he cannot do. Drucker argues that the practice of lifetime employment has enabled Japanese companies to take the long view (twenty-five years) in developing managers and so explains why despite all expectations, Japanese companies pro-duce strong leaders:

> The house of Mitsui is the oldest of the world's big businesses. It dates back to 1637, half a century before the Bank of England was founded . . . In the more than three hundred years of its business life, Mitsui has never had a chief executive (the Japanese term is "chief banto' - literally, chief clerk) who was not an outstanding man and powerful leader. This accomplishment is not matched by any other institution, whether the Catholic Church, any government, army, navy, university, or corporation . . .
>
> At first sight nothing would seem less likely to develop strong executives than the Japanese system. It would seem, rather, to be the ideal prescription for developing timid men selected for proven mediocrity and trained not to rock the boat . . .
>
> It is precisely *because* (italics Drucker's) Japanese managers have life-time employment and can as a rule, be neither fired nor moved, and *because* (italics Drucker's) advancement for the first twenty-five years of a man's working life is through seniority alone that the Japanese have made the care and feeding of their young people the first responsibility of top management.[17]

In the research design of the Negandhi study, the objective of making the local firms in the developing countries comparable to the American and Japanese subsidiaries was on the basis of industry, size, technology and product mix, the basic assumption being that similar companies in the same industry would pursue the same strategy and should therefore have the same structure. Such as-sumption is not tenable. The companies could not be expected to have identical competitive positions (i.e. American subsidiaries are able to draw on support from the parent company while Taiwan firms look to the Taiwan government for support) and so could not be expected to pursue the same strategy and to establish the same structure.

Thus, the difference in the management practices followed by the Chinese firms may be attributed to both the strategy they are pursuing as well as to the corporate culture (i.e. Chinese) under which they operate in. Howard H. Stevenson of the Harvard Busi-ness School provides a framework which would explain the struc-ture of the Chinese Managerial System.

C. *The Structure of the Chinese Managerial System*

In a paper entitled, "A New Paradigm for Entrepreneurial Management,"[18] Howard H. Stevenson seeks to define Entrepreneurial Management in terms of individual or corporate behavior. In terms of examining individual or corporate behavior, Stevenson suggests that the approach be to consider a range or spectrum of behavior that runs from the "promoter" (the type who says, "I can make it happen") to the "trustee" (the type who says, "I must guard what I have"). While the entrepreneur is not identical to the promoter, he occupies a range on the promoter end of the spectrum. Likewise, while the administrator is not identical to the trustee, he occupies a range on the trustee end of the spectrum. Stevenson then relates his suggested paradigm to the five key dimensions of business that are traditionally elements of general management: the strategic orientation, the commitment to opportunity, the commitment of resources, the control of resources and the management structure. The result is presented in Figure VI-6.

My contention is that the structure of the Chinese Managerial System is not *entrepreneurial or administrative* but rather *entrepreneurial and administrative*. Such a duality of structure can be traced to the strong belief of Chinese businessmen that entrepreneurship is a family or stockholder function while admistration can be a professional management function.

Whether the Chinese Managerial System necessarily implies family ownership or control or whether like the Japanese Managerial System is capable of evolving into a public corporation with a strong entrepreneurial orientation is a debatable issue. However, one of my most significant findings has been the attainment of multinational status by several Chinese firms **without** yielding family control. In a sense therefore, such achievement renders academic the issue of whether family ownership is a necessary component of the Chinese managerial system.

To understand how such a difficult achievement could have been accomplished, one should note the obstacles that face such an undertaking:

1) If the top management of a company can only be drawn from members of a family or even a clan, this policy automatically reduces the pool of available talent.

2) Even if this talent is available from the family, there is no assurance that the most qualified member of the family will be chosen for the top management position.

3) Even if this talent is available, and even if it were chosen for the top position, there is still the need to place untalented members of the family in some managerial positions. This move would

FIGURE VI-6
A PARADIGM FOR ENTREPRENEURIAL MANAGEMENT

Promoter	Key business dimension	Trustee
Driven by perception of opportunity	Entrepreneurial Domain ←→ Managerial Domain ←→ Strategic Orientation	Driven by resources currently controlled
Revolutionary with short duration	Entrepreneurial Domain ←→ Managerial Domain ←→ Commitment to Opportunity	Evolutionary of long duration
Multistaged with minimal exposure at each stage	Entrepreneurial Domain ←→ Managerial Domain ←→ Commitment to Resources	Single-staged with complete commitment upon decision
Episodic use or rent of required resources	Entrepreneurial Domain ←→ Managerial Domain ←→ Control of Resources	Ownership or employment of required resources
Flat with multiple informal networks	Entrepreneurial Domain ←→ Managerial Domain ←→ Management Structure	Formalized hierarchy

Source: Howard H. Stevenson, "A New Paradigm for Entrepreneurial Management," Harbard Business School, Working Paper, 1984, p. 32.

have adverse effects on employee morale and on the overall efficiency of the firm and so place the firm at a competitive disadvantage with the publicly-owned firms.

Several Chinese firms have overcome such obstacles by:
1) Focusing on one key mangerial function, entrepreneurship. Thus the limited pool of talent is not expected to excel in all aspects of management. Only in one.
2) Focusing on entrepreneurship simplifies the management development program of the Chinese firms to that which develops entrepreneurs from among the family and assures their ascension to the top management position.

3) Placing the less talented family members in managerial positions which are primarily of custodial or control nature (i.e. treasury, purchasing, warehousing, etc.). Their competitive advantage (family trust and loyalty) can be brought to bear on such positions.

That the Chinese family firms have chosen to focus on entrepreneurship as their area of expertise can be justified on several grounds:
1) The experience and the expertise of the founding fathers has been in entrepreneurship.
2) The number of entrepreneurs which a business firm needs to survive are much less than the number of required professional managers.
3) The chances of hiring entrepreneurial managers are quite low. In fact, one Chinese businessman flatly asserted, "Professional managers you can hire, entrepreneurs you cannot."
4) The development of entrepreneurs is one area (as compared to technology, for example) where the Western multinationals hold no competitive advantage.

The decision of the Chinese to focus on entrepreneurship is evident in all the case studies of Chinese industrialists previously presented. Let us examine in greater detail three Chinese industrialist groups - Bangkok Bank, the Liem Group and the Astra Group - to illustrate the range of variations inthe structure of the Chinese Managerial System.

D. Case Studies on the Chinese Managerial System

The success of Bangkok Bank has been attributed to the acute business instinct of Chin Sophonpanich and the administrative genius of Boonchu Rojanasathien.[19]

When Chin Sophonpanich took over the management of Bangkok Bank in 1952, he had already made his mark as a Chinese entrepreneur. Born on June 24, 1910 in Thonburi, Thailand, Chin Sophonpanich (also known as Tang Piak Chin) was the son of a Teochiu commercial clerk. Educated in China, Chin returned to Thailand at the age of seventeen and settled down. After working at several trades, he became a clerk in a construction company and rose to the post of assistant manager at the age of twenty. After fire closed down the firm in 1931, Chin became a manager of Siem Heng Long Co. Ltd., a dealer in construction materials. In 1935, at the age of twenty-five, Chin started his own trading company, Asia Trading Co. Ltd. which dealt in lumber, hardware and canned goods. During the Second World War, Chin expanded his operations by exporting rice to Indonesia and by integrating into the operation of saw mills. By the end of the war, Chin had amassed enough capital and experience acting as *comprador* (middleman) to the foreign banks to join with several Thai businessmen in organizing Bangkok Bank in 1944. While active in the board, Chin was not involved in the management of the bank during its early years. During this period, Chin expanded into a number of businesses including shipping, insurance, contracting and ice manufacturing in addition to continuing his import-export operations. In 1952, Bangkok Bank experienced difficulties because of the mismanagement of the business associates of Chin. In the reorganization that followed, Chin assumed active management of the bank.

Boochu Rojanasathien, an accountant by profession, joined Bangkok Bank at the invitation of Chin as internal auditor. Boonchu's initial assignment (in fact his initial contract was a temporary one) was to set up the internal control systems so as to prevent a recurrence of the liquidity problems which the bank encountered. Under Boonchu's administrative leadership, the bank built up its managerial organization by recruiting professional managers such as Damrong Krishnamara (in charge of control), Vira Ramyarupa (a lawyer in charge of the domestic branch network), Piya Sivayathorn (in charge of domestic credit), and John C. Cheung (a former Bank of America manager in charge of international operations). In addition, the bank developed a corp of specialists in banking ranging from foreign exchange specialists (i.e currency traders) to credit specialists (i.e. agriculture). For the lower management levels, Boonchu instituted a vigourous personnel development programme. Confirmation of his managerial performance came in the form of his appointment to the presidency of the Bangkok Bank. In addition, his administrative services were called upon by the government of Thailand in terms of cabinet appointments: as Minister of Finance in 1975 and as Deputy Prime Minister (economic czar) in 1980.

It may of course be argued that this partnership is the result of fortuitous coincidences. Even if this were so, the new management at the helm of Bangkok Bank where Chatri Sophonpanich, the second son of Chin Sophonpanich is the president and Amnuay Viravan, a professional manager is the Chairman of the Executive Committee (Chin Sophonpanich remains as the Chairman of the Board) indicates that the bank intends to continue this successful formula.

That Chatri, the second son was chosen over the first son, Robin, indicates a more deliberative selection process than that of primogeniture. That Chatri was chosen over the more professionally trained son, Chote, would indicate criteria other than professional management experience and banking expertise. Chote Sophonpanich, an Economics graduate from the University of Sydney, was considered a respected banker with long experience in international banking. In recognition of such experience in banking, he became chairman of ASEAN Finance Corporation. His management credentials include membership in the Planning and Development Committee of Thammasat University as well as his position as Councilor of the Thai Management Association.

Chatri Sophonpanich, on the other hand, is credited with possessing one particular gift similar to that of his father; a sharp business sense highlighted by the ability to identify new marketing opportunities. As proof of his entrepreneurial acumen, Chatri had personally amassed a portfolio of profitable investments in several Thai companies. While Chatri received some training in banking from the Royal Bank of Scotland, his primary exposure has been in entrepreneurship. His father's contacts with the regional Overseas Chinese tycoons have been passed on to him. Moreover, like his father, Chatri has established strong links with the power center of Thai politics, the Thai military. Chatri Sophonpanich is a personal associate of army commander-in-chief General Arthit Kamlang-ek, considered one of the most powerful figure in Thailand.

While Chatri Sophonpanich was trained to be entrepreneur, Amnuay Viravan was educated as a professional manager and served as a rising government technocrat in the ministry of finance. After receiving his undergraduate degree (Bachelor of Commerce) at Chulalongkorn University in Thailand, Viravan went to the University of Michigan for two masters degrees (M.B.A. and M. A. Economics) and a doctorate degree (Ph.D. Bus. Adm.). After serving as Economic Adviser to the Prime Minister of Thailand for nine years (1962-1971), Viravan was appointed to a staff position in the Ministry of National Development (Director of the Technical and Planning Department). From that position he rose steadily in the Thai civil service, becoming Permanent Secretary for Finance in 1977. In 1980, he was finally appointed Minister of Finance under the then Deputy Prime Minister Boonchu Rojanasathien. In 1983, Amnuay Viravan was handpicked by Chin Sophonpanich and approved by Chatri Sophonpanich for the position of senior executive adviser and executive director of Bangkok Bank.

In the case of the Soeryadjaya Group in Indonesia, the same teaming up between the entrepreneur and the professional manager occurred.[20] In the words of William Soeryadjaya, "The key factor in whatever I have achieved is that I always knew my weakness. I am not an administrator." In 1972, sensing that his business organization, which had grown significantly, needed administrative support, Soeryadjaya hired a finance executive from Holland, A. L. Vijverberg, formerly an executive of Hoechst, who established the financial reporting and auditing systems of the Astra Group of companies. In terms of the management team of Astra, Soeryadjaya established close links with several training institutes such as IN-SEAD, Stanford, the Asian Institute of Management and Indonesia's Institute for Management. These institutes have assisted in the training of the Astra managers and in setting up management programs (i.e. Japanese-type Quality Control Circles and Western-style Management by Objective).

By 1983, the management structure of the Astra Group had three distinct components:

1) A Board of Commissioners consisting of William Soeryadjaya (chairman and founder), Lily Soeryadjaya (wife and treasurer), Edward Soeryadjaya (eldest son), Judith Tan (daughter), Joyce Soeryadjaya (daughter) and Paul Lapian (the only non-family member) which is responsible for the entrepreneurial decisions of the Astra group (i.e. whether or not to invest in agribusiness);

2) A Management Group headed by Benjamin Suriadjaya (a younger brother of William Soeryadjaya) operating under a participative management culture and a decentralized type of organization; and

3) A team of three Dutch administration executives who act as consultant to the Board of Commissioners and to the Management Group.

In both the Sophonpanich and the Soeryadjaya Group the distinction between the entrepreneurial and the managerial functions may be conceptually clear but organizationally blurred. In the case of the Liem Group, the organizational distinction is also clear.[21] The entrepreneurial organization consists of the Indonesian companies (Liem's onshore business empire) while the managerial organization consists of the non-Indonesian companies (Liem's offshore business empire).

Liem's offshore business empire has been built through the most modern and sophisticated form of managerial capitalism, the acquisition in the stock market of established companies in Hong Kong, the Dutch Netherland and the United States. In 1982 the Liems took over Shanghai Land a Hong Kong company whose principal assets are its public listing in the Hong Kong Stock Exchange and its heritage as a company organized in 1888 to do business in Shanghai, China. Using Shanghai Land (renamed First Pacific Holdings) as the investment vehicle, the Liems acquired control of two other venerable institutions, Hagemeyer, a ninety year old Dutch trading company, and Hibernia, a California bank (the 12th biggest in California at the time of its acquisition). The elements of the strategy behind such moves would be as follows:

1) The investments outside Indonesia would provide some political diversification for the Liem Group.

2) The acquisition of established organizations in international trading and banking provides a natural connection with the group's Indonesian operations. There are all sorts of Indonesian raw materials Hagemeyer can ship to Europe and the United States, as well as finished goods from those countries to Indonesia (i.e. the trader strategy on an international scale). In addition to providing access to the U. S. capital markets, Hibernia Bank could handle the trade financing for Hagemeyer. Hibernia, for instance, handles Indonesia's wheat imports (i.e Bogasari Flour Mills [owned by the Liem Group]) worth around US$ 330 million a year.

What is noteworthy about the Liems' offshore empire is that the management is completely professional. The Hong Kong operations are headed by Manuel Pangilinan, a Filipino formerly with Amex Bank in Hong Kong. The second in command is Robert Meyer, an American lawyer. The rest of the management are Hong Kong Chinese professional managers. The Dutch managers at Hagemeyer and the American managers at Hibernia Bank were kept in place. There is, however no question that the person the Liem family assigned to oversee the offshore operations is Anthony Salim, Liem's youngest son and heir-apparent.

There are several reasons for such a dual structure:
1) As stated earlier, the Indonesian companies operating as institutionalized business deals do not require professional management. Moreover, as they have been performing satisfactorily, there is less incentive to risk disrupting the system.
2) The technical aspects of the operations can easily be handled by the hiring of foreign technicians while the business aspects (trading, distribution, credit system) require reliance on Chinese agents or family managers.
3) On the other hand, the offshore businesses require both the credibility and competence of professional managers.
4) The present structure provides the Liem Group with extreme flexibility in terms of choosing the specific managerial system for specific business projects.

In summary then, the structure of the Chinese Managerial System consists of the following:
1) An entrepreneurial group consisting of the family;
2) A professional management group consisting primarily of professional managers;
3) A custodial group which performs the control function for the entrepreneurial group over the professional management group and which consists primarily of family members and trusted retainers.

FIGURE UI-7
ORGANIZATIONAL STRUCTURE OF THE CHINESE
MANAGERIAL SYSTEM

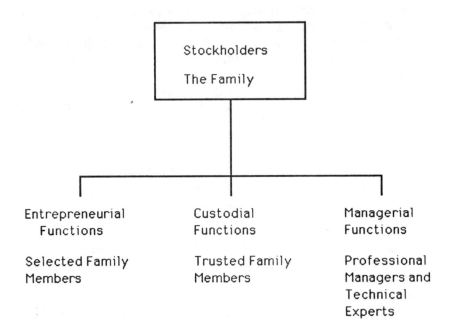

Figure VI-7 shows the typical structure of a large-scale Chinese business group.

E. *Management Development under the Chinese Managerial System*

In view of the willingness of the Overseas Chinese to subcontract the managerial function to professional managers, as well as their willingness to encourage and support in-house training programs for their employees, they have been able to focus on their distinctive competence: the education and development of entrepreneurs. This section will therefore provide in broad outline the entrepreneurial development program as evolved by the Overseas Chinese businessmen.[23]

The Chinese believe that "A father cannot teach his son, but neither should a stranger teach one's son." Underlying this saying is the belief that teaching is a combination of affection, expertise, and objectivity. The emotional aspects of a father-son relationship may so becloud a father's perception that his expertise is rendered useless while the purely commercial aspect of a son entails the risk of unconcern and inattention. Thus, the usual teacher of a budding Chinese entrepreneur could be a good friend or a close relative of the father.

The educational program that the Chinese have evolved in the development of entrepreneurs consists of three successive stages; the progression from one stage to the next dictated by the learning pace of the student rather than the time deadlines of the teacher.[23] The stages are: the total immersion stage, the tutorial stage, and the walkabout stage.

During the total immersion stage, the budding entrepreneur is assigned purely to sales of a clerical nature or even to menial tasks with no managerial or business responsibilities whatsoever. Pedagogically, learning is best achieved from a lowly rather than a vantage position, for the powers of observation are most enhanced from a position of powerlessness. (Thus the basis for that statement that the weak are the most acute of observers.) The sharpened powers of observation of the budding entrepreneurs should lead to the following results:

1) A mastery of the "nitty-gritty" of business. This initial bonding into business reality should henceforth leaven whatever wild business ideas, the budding entrepreneur may have in the future with the litmus test of practicability.

2) An observation of the unfairness of business life. Some people succeed, some people fail. Results, not efforts are rewarded by the business organization.

3) A realization of the great disparity in work satisfaction and financial compensation between the entrepreneur and the non-entrepreneur. The Chinese devoutly believe that a large gap should exist between the entrepreneur-owner and the employee-manager. They see this as a strong incentive for their young people to aspire to be entrepreneurs. Our budding entrepreneurs will surely become aware of what they and the managers for the owner are paid as compared to what the owner earns.

4) An admiration for the owner-entrepreneur who is in control, who orchestrates everything, and who defines the rules and regulations without being subject to them.

By the time the budding entrepreneur graduates to the second stage of the entrepreneurial development program, he would have demonstrated a grasp of business reality and a driving ambition to succeed.

The tutorial stage of the entrepreneurial development program starts when the mentor brings the budding entrepreneur along with him to his business meetings. As described earlier, the Chinese businessman is basically a deal maker. A deal is a complete business transaction at the end of which a businessman can usually determine whether or not a profit has been made. The entrepreneurial student is usually taken along by his mentors to observe a deal from start to finish. Being of no consequence to the consummation of the deal, he is allowed to observe how a deal is actually developed and consummated. At any stage in the deal-making process, his tutor may question him about his understanding of the deal while he in turn may ask his teacher about the rationale and logic of certain moves being made by all the parties to the deal. Again, from the pedagogical viewpoint, this is the most effective learning mode for several reasons:

1) the student to teacher ratio is one-to-one;
2) the learning process is experiential rather than abstract;
3) the feedback is immediate, frequent and clear;
4) the results are not pre-ordained, thus providing an element of suspense and excitement;
5) the level of interest is high and the focus of attention all-consuming; and
6) the lessons are abstracted from the student's observations and not predigested by the teacher.

After the student-entrepreneur goes through the observation of, and eventually even partial participation in, several deals, his teacher may decide that he is ready for the final stage in the entrepreneurial development process, the Chinese Walkabout. The term walkabout is derived from a rite of passage into adulthood undertaken by Australian aborigines.[24]

The budding entrepreneur must pass through a similar rite of passage. He must generate, nurse, and consummate a business deal successfully. All that he has learned must now be applied successfully to an actual business situation. The final arbiter of his success or failure will not be his teacher but rather the impersonal business forces surrounding him.

To fund his business deal, the budding entrepreneur could approach his mentor, his family, his clan association or even the Chinese Chamber of Commerce. These social organizations perform the role performed more formally by the venture companies in the United States. In the spirit of venture companies, the project and the proponent are evaluated. However, in the end, the budding entrepreneur will most likely obtain his financing secured only by postdated checks (a Chinese business practice discussed earlier).

As in the Australian walkabout, once the Chinese entrepreneur begins his walkabout, there are only two possible outcomes. If the deal succeeds (the postdated checks do not bounce), he is welcomed as a new member of the Chinese business community, tested by the fire of business adversity and ready to make his contribution to the economic growth and influence of his community. If the first deal fails (the postdated checks bounce), the budding entrepreneur may be given another opportunity to prove that the first was merely bad luck. If he fails again, the Chinese business community concludes that he has no claim to the economic resources of the community. He is denied access to credit, without which no business man can survive.

The judgment of the business community may be harsh and the educational process unforgiving, but the entrepreneurial principles have been repeatedly espoused by management experts. Do not continue subsidizing losers. Focus your resources (time and money) on the proven winners, for only by doing so will you create sufficient economic activity to enable you to place even those who failed the supreme entrepreneurial test as professional managers or even custodians in your business organizations.

It is of course from this pool of seasoned entrepreneurs that Chinese business groups select which family member will be chosen to head the group, thus creating a more effective mode of management succession.

E. *The Chinese Managerial System in ASEAN*

In summary then, the Chinese Managerial System in ASEAN can now be placed in relation to other managerial systems. If these systems are classified into two major group; Western and Eastern, the Chinese managerial system in ASEAN would fall under the Eastern managerial system group. Thus, in comparison to the Western system which is individual-oriented and based on impersonal relationships in the workplace, the Chinese system in ASEAN is an Eastern system which is group-oriented and based on interpersonal relationships in the workplace.

In contrast to other Eastern managerial systems such as the Japanese which relies on professional managers for both entrepreneurship and administration, the Chinese managerial system in ASEAN is classified under the Chinese managerial system which relies on the family to perform the entrepreneurial function and on professional managers to perform the administrative functions. (The Korean managerial system is in transition from the family corporation (business group type) to the public corporation (Japanese group type)[25]. Lastly, the Chinese managerial system in ASEAN (except Singapore) is distinguished by its commodity orientation and its business strategy of turnover (low-margin and high volume) in comparison to the Chinese managerial system in East Asia with its production-orientation and its business strategy of focusing on labor-intensive products for the markets of the developed countries[26]. (Singapore has elements of both.) Figure VI-8 presents the typology we have just discussed.

FIGURE UI-8
A TYPOLOGY OF MANAGERIAL SYSTEMS

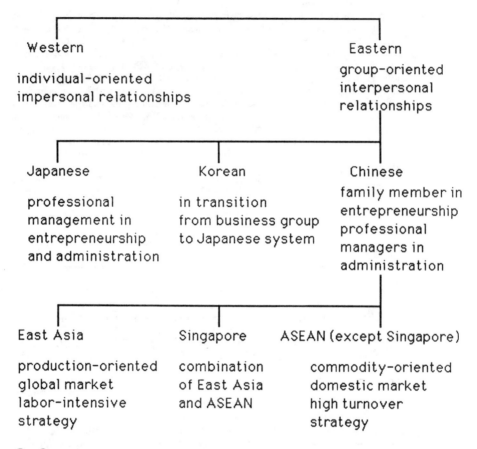

Western

individual-oriented
impersonal relationships

Eastern

group-oriented
interpersonal
relationships

Japanese

professional
management in
entrepreneurship
and administration

Korean

in transition
from business group
to Japanese system

Chinese

family member in
entrepreneurship
professional
managers in
administration

East Asia

production-oriented
global market
labor-intensive
strategy

Singapore

combination
of East Asia
and ASEAN

ASEAN (except Singapore)

commodity-oriented
domestic market
high turnover
strategy

G. *Summary*

The Chinese managerial system, as part of the Asian managerial system, shares with the Japanaese and the Korean managerial system the corporate values of group orientation and close interpersonal relationship based on respect for authority. This system has been fashioned to implement the distinct business strategies of the Overseas Chinese. It is these distinct business strategies, acting on the Chinese culture of the Overseas Chinese in the ASEAN region, which have created the distinguishing characteristics of the Chinese managerial system in the ASEAN region: family control of the business, focus on entrepreneurship as the distinct area of family competence, astute placement of non-entrepreneurial family members in custodial positions and a willingness to delegate to professional managers the administrative functions of the business.

NOTES

1. S. G. Redding, "Cognition as an Aspect of Culture and its Relation to Management Processes: An Exploratory View of the Chinese," *Journal of Management Studies*, May 1980, Volume 17, Number 2, pp. 127-148.
2. Ibid., p. 147. An example of a large-scale but personally managed business group that fits Redding's description would be the Chang Group. Chang Ming Chien, a Malaysian Chinese built a business empire stretching from Hong Kong, to Taiwan, to the Philippines, to Indonesia, to Singapore, to Malaysia and to Thailand. Upon his sudden death, the business empire collapsed. For a detailed description of this business group, see Gary Coull, "A giant spiderless web," *Far Eastern Economic Review*, June 11, 1982, pp. 105-108.
3. "The New Multinationals," *Business in Thailand*, September 1983, pp. 19-21. Historically the first Chinese firm which could be considered multinational was the Kian Gwan Company founded by Oei Tjie Sien in Indonesia in 1863, which flourished until its nationalization by the government of Sukarno in 1961. For a detailed history of the company, see J. Panglaykim and I. Palmer, "Study of Entrepreneurship in Developing Countries: The Development of One Chinese Concern in Indonesia," *Journal of Southeast Asian Studies*, March 1970, pp. 85-95.
4. See, for example, Milan Kubr and John Wallace, *Successes and Failures in Meeting the Management Challenge: Strategies and their Implementation*, (Washington, D. C.: The World Bank, 1983).
5. Anant R. Negandhi and S. Benjamin Prasad, *Comparative Management*, (New York: Appleton-Century-Crofts, 1971). For a more detailed discussion of this issue, see Limlingan, "Professional Management in Developing Countries," Unpublished mimeograph, 1985.
6. Louis T. Wells, *Third World Multinationals: The Rise of Foreign Investment from Developing Countries*, (Cambridge: The Massachusetts Institute of Technology Press, 1983). See also K. Kumar and M. G. Mcleod, *Multinationals from Developing Countries*, (Lexington, MA: Lexington Books, 1981).
7. Related articles by Redding on the Chinese managerial system are: "Bridging the Culture Gap," *Asian Business and Industry*, April 1978, pp. 48-51; "What makes a Chinese business tick?," *Asian Business and Industry*, March 1979, pp. 68-72; "Culture clash on the factory floor," *Asian Business and Industry*, May 1979, pp. 66-68; "Cultural effects on the marketing process in Southeast Asia," *Journal of the Market Research Society*, Volume 24, Number 2, 1982, pp. 98-114; Western and Chinese mode of reasoning and their implications for engineering management," *Hong Kong Engineer*, March 1982, pp. 26-28; and "Management Education for Orientals," unidentified publication.
8. S. G. Redding and Michael Ng, "The Role of 'Face' in the Organizational Perceptions of Chinese Managers," *Organizational Studies*, 1982, Volume 3, Number 3, pp. 201-219.
9. Geert Hofstede, "Motivation, Leadership and Organization: Do American Theories Apply Abroad?," *Organizational Dynamics*, Summer 1980, pp. 42-62.
10. Ibid., Figure 6, p. 52.
11. Hall, *Beyond Culture*, (New York: Anchor Press, 1976).
12. Redding, pp. 146-147.
13. Geert Hofstede, "The Cultural Relativity of Organizational Practices and Theories," *Journal of International Business Studies*, Fall 1983.
14. Anant R. Negandhi, *Management and Economic Development: The Case of Taiwan*, (The Hague: Martinus Nijhoff, 1973).
15. Peter Drucker, *Management: Tasks, Responsibilities, Practices*, (New York: Harper & Row, Publishers, 1974), pp. 465-480.
16. Ibid., p. 465.
17. Ibid., pp. 254-255.
18. Howard H. Stevenson, "A New Paradigm for Entrepreneurial Management," *Harvard Business School*, Working Paper, 1984.
19. The Chinese family is of course an extended family (i.e. children, relatives and in-laws) and therefore could draw on more resources than the comparable Western family. For descriptions on the extended Chinese family in business, see John T. Omohundro,

"Social Networks and Business Success for the Philippine Chinese," in Lim and Gosling. *The Chinese in Southeast Asia: Ethnicity and Economic Activity.*

20. For published sources on Bangkok Bank, Chin Sophonpanich, Boonchu Rojanasathien, Chatri Sophonpanich, and Amnuay Viravan see Note 29 of Chapter five.

21. For published sources on William Soeryadjaya and the Astra Group, see Note 14 of Chapter five.

22. For published sources on Liem Sioe Liong and the Liem Group, see Notes 12 and 13 of Chapter five.

23. This section is based on a paper I wrote. (Limlingan, "The Chinese Walkabout: A Case Study in Entrepreneurial Education," *Asian Institute of Management*, Occasional Paper, 1983.) For a more sociological approach see Burton Benedict, "Family Firms and Firm Families: A Comparison of Indian, Chinese, and Creole Firms in Seychelles," in Sydney Greenfield, Arnold Strickon and Robert Aubey, *Entrepreneurs in Cultural Context*, (Albuquerque, New Mexico: University of New Mexico Press, 1979).

24. For a similar description of entrepreneurial training, see John L. Espy, "Case Study: Hong Kong Textiles, Ltd.," in John L. Espy, "The Strategies of Chinese Industrial Enterprises in Hong Kong," *Harvard Business School*, Unpublished DBA Thesis, June 1970, pp. 238-267.

25. Among Australian aborigines, before a boy can be accepted as an adult, he must undertake a six-month long endurance test during which he must survive alone - in the wilderness and return to his tribe an adult or die in the attempt. He thus faces a severe but extremely appropriate trial in which he must demonstrate the knowledge he has learned in an environment which does not take his effort into consideration and is capricious, fickle, and unfair.

26. For a study of Korean business groups, see Seok Ki Kim, "Chaebol in Korean Environment: Samsung Group - Its Entrepreneurial History, Sources of Expansion, and Evolution of Structure and Scope," Unpublished mimeograph, 1984; "Growth of Chaebol in Korea: Government, Market, and Entrepreneurship," Unpublished mimeograph, 1985 and "Business Concentration and Government Policy: A Study of the Phenomenon of Business Groups," *Harvard Business School*, forthcoming DBA Thesis.

27. For a description of the business strategies of Chinese firms in Hong Kong, see John L. Espy, "The Strategies of Chinese Industrial Enterprises in Hong Kong," *Harvard Business School*, Unpublished DBA Thesis, June 1970. For the finding that Chinese firms in East Asia have maintained the function of entrepreneurship within the family and still developed sophisticated production systems, see Wenlee Ting, *Business and Technological Dynamics in Newly Industrializing Asia*, (Westport, Connecticut: Quorum Books, 1985).

CHAPTER VII
SUMMARY

In Chapter one, I stated as my major research interest the formulation of a conceptual framework for explaining how the Overseas Chinese in the ASEAN region have achieved such a remarkable economic performance. In this chapter, I propose to state my thesis in a series of propositions.

1. **The remarkable economic performance of the Overseas Chinese in the ASEAN is fact and** *cannot* **be explained away by any statistical or structural hypothesis.**

   While constituting only six per cent of the population of the ASEAN countries, the Overseas Chinese are estimated to have a much greater share of the economic activities of the ASEAN countries. In addition to the economic statistics there are several indicators for this assertion. The largest private commercial bank in ASEAN is a Thai Chinese bank, Bangkok Bank. The largest private agribusiness firm in ASEAN is a Thai Chinese firm, Charoen Pokphand. The two largest business groups in Indonesia are Indonesian Chinese, the Liem Group and the Soeryadjaya Group.

   Moreover, this economic performance cannot be attributed to a small group among the Chinese minority. Available statistics indicate that the income distribution of the Chinese is more statistically normal as compared to other racial groups. Nor can such economic performance be attributed to accidents of geography (i.e. the Chinese preferring to live in the urban areas). Attempts to close the income gap between the Chinese and the indigenous population by restructuring these external factors have met with little success.

2. **The remarkable performance of the Overseas Chinese** *cannot* **be explained by the Trader hypothesis which assumes that the Overseas Chinese who came to ASEAN were already traders trained in commercial operations and funded by substantial capital.**

   The popular myth that the Chinese arrived as traders trained in commercial operations and funded by substantial capital is not validated by historical analysis. The great majority of the Chinese who came to the ASEAN countries came as coolie laborers drawn from the peasant class and reared in a society which at that time possessed neither the commercial skills nor inclinations of the Overseas Chinese. Rather than bring capital to the region, the primary objective of the coolie laborers was the remittance of funds to their families in China.

3. The rejection of the trader hypothesis requires a hypothesis which would explain how Chinese businessmen evolved from the mass migration of coolie laborers and without capital support either from China or from their country of residence.

If the Overseas Chinese arrived in the ASEAN countries with no built-in advantage, they did not derive any advantage whatsoever from their countries of residence. On the contrary, they had to expect the enactment of policies which would further handicap them. Hypotheses explaining their remarkable economic performance solely to their immigrant origins, minority status, Chinese culture or to the ASEAN economic environment fail the test of empirical reality. If they succeeded simply because they were immigrants, then why were other immigrant groups not as successful as they were? If they succeeded simply because they were a minority group, then why did the Singapore Chinese, who are a majority in their country, also succeed? (This also holds for the Chinese in Hong Kong and Taiwan.) If they succeeded simply because they were Chinese, why were the Chinese not successful in their own homeland? If they succeeded simply because of the ASEAN economic environment, why did the indigenous population who were in the same environment not succeed? The inevitable attribution of their economic success to a combination of their immigrant origins, their minority status, their Chinese culture and the ASEAN economic environment is met by the inevitable question of why such a combination should result in superior economic performance.

4. My hypothesis for explaining the remarkable economic performance of the Overseas Chinese in ASEAN is based on the business policy framework of a superior strategy effectively implemented by a structure flowing from the strategy and consistent with Chinese culture.

The hypothesis which would explain why and how is based on the business policy framework. This framework is ideally suited for two reasons. For one, the phenomenon under study is a business phenomenon and should therefore be more appropriately defined within a business framework. For another, the framework is premised on the assumption that a combination of factors such as the environment, the corporate culture and the firm's resources require the formulation of a distinct strategy and structure. My hypothesis is that the Overseas Chinese in ASEAN have discovered such a strategy and have devised the corresponding structure.

5. The superior business strategy of the Overseas Chinese is actually a series of strategies based on creating and sustaining superior performance.

a) A low-margin/high-volume strategy aimed at achieving significant market shares.

Using the Chinese community as a resource base, Chinese businessmen have focused on performing the intermediation function for the developing economies of the ASEAN countries. As entry strategy, they have foregone the economic surplus of their more efficient intermediation effort by accepting a margin lower than what the market expects. This entry strategy has several advantages. It eases whatever ill-will their presence may create in the indigenous population, forces out less efficient competitors and masks the enormous profits which the resulting high turnover may make possible. More importantly, the strategy allows the Chinese businessman to achieve a significant share of the market.

b) Achievement of significant market share, pursuing a strategy based on economies of scope.

Several strategies based on economies of scope are available to the Chinese businessman. He could handle additional products for the same market (i.e. buying the corn as well as the rice from the group of farmers). He could increase the range of his services to the same market (i.e. milling the rice for the farmer). He could limit the investment required to service his present market (i.e. paying for purchases of rice with fertilizer). He could reduce the cost of servicing his present market (i.e. using his trucks to carry rice to the city and returning them loaded with farm supplies for the farmers).

c) Achievement of economies of scale, pursuing an opportunistic strategy of exploring and exploiting business opportunities in the form of business deals.

Business opportunities in developing countries usually arise because of imperfect information, inadequate infrastructure and lack of credit facilities. The Chinese businessman, through the Chinese Trading Company which has been structured for sustaining and making business deals, enjoys a distinct advantage. His information is cost-free, a by-product of his trading operation. His infrastructure (company and Chinese community) is far superior to the outside infrastructure. His access to credit from suppliers and Chinese community is far greater than that of his non-Chinese competitors.

d) Establishment of an organization and the raising of adequate capital through accumulated profits from operations and from successful business deals, the formulation of a more specific strategy largely shaped by the economic development policies of the ASEAN countries.

In Indonesia and the Philippines, the economic development policy of industrialization through import-substitution and the nationalistic policies forcing the divestiture of Chinese trading activities dictated a business strategy based on shifting from trading to manufacturing while retaining the trading preference for making money on business deals rather than operations.

In Malaysia, the New Economic Policy of the government, dictated a strategy based on political support and maintaining the Chinese share in the overall economic pie. This meant acquisition of the publicly traded British company and bidding for the economic projects being undertaken by the government.

In Thailand, the government adopted an economic development strategy based on agricultural development and a policy of Chinese assimilation. The two public policies allowed the Thai Chinese businessmen to pursue strategies based on the agricultural resource base of the country and on the existing business base of the Chinese community.

In Singapore, the government adopted an economic development strategy to continue as the entrepot and financial center of Southeast Asia while at the same time establishing an industrial base that is internationally competitive. Guided by such policies, the Singaporean Chinese businessmen have followed the traditional strategy of intermediation (i.e. banking) while exploring new alternative intermediation strategies (i.e joint venture).

In Brunei, the government focused on the wise management of its primary resource, oil. This strategy provided no opportunity for the Chinese businessmen in Brunei to advance from traders to industrialists.

6. **The effective structure devised by the Overseas Chinese in ASEAN was built on their twin areas of strength: entrepreneurship and the Chinese culture.**

   a) The use of social-control systems to offset the lack of Western-type control systems.

   The Chinese businessman has traditionally used the cash-flow system of accounting in contrast to the double-entry system. Its simplicity has also meant an inadequate control system. The Chinese solution is to rely on social control (i.e. family ties) to augment the weak formal control system. In addition, Chinese firms have relied on their own social organizations (the Chinese Chamber of Commerce as credit bureau) and on their social customs (payment of debt during the Chinese New Year), and even on the modern commercial banking system (postdated checks) to facilitate their business operations.

   b) The adoption of an entrepreneurial organization which in its opportunistic orientation is appropriate in a developing country environment.

Under the Stevenson paradigm, the Chinese trading company is driven by perception of opportunity rather than by resources currently controlled; its commitment to opportunity, revolutionary with short duration rather than evolutionary and of long duration; its commitment of resources, multistaged with minimal exposure at each stage rather than single-staged with complete commitment upon decision; its control of resources of episodic use, or rented rather than owned; and its management structure flat with multiple informal networks rather than a formalized hierarchy.

c) The focus on the function of entrepreneurship in terms of the role of the chief executive, the training of family members in entrepreneurship and the selection of future successors on the basis of entrepreneurial qualities.

As illustrated by our cases studies on Bangkok Bank, the Astra Group and the Liem Group, the decision of the Chinese industrialist to focus on the entrepreneurial function have resulted in the willingness to delegate the administrative functions to professional managers so long as the organization is directed by an entrepreneur from the family. The focus on entrepreneurship has also allowed Chinese business to concentrate on the training and development of entrepreneurs. As noted, the effectiveness of their training system for entrepreneurship is comparable to that presently being undertaken in the more formal schools of management. Moreover, such entrepreneurship is of great interest to the participants as succession in the Chinese Managerial System is based on entrepreneurial, not managerial capabilities. Lastly, the Chinese Managerial System shows astuteness in placing non-entrepreneurial family members in custodial positions.

CHAPTER VIII
AREAS FOR FURTHER RESEARCH

In this book, I have proposed a business policy framework which would best explain, as compared to other suggested frameworks, the economic success of the Overseas Chinese in the ASEAN region. Considering that such a proposal has not yet been subjected to test in the marketplace of ideas, we would expect as further areas of research the following:
1) Validation of the magnitude and scope of the economic success of the Overseas Chinese;
2) Validation of past and present business strategies employed by the Overseas Chinese;
3) Validation of the presence and pervasiveness of the Chinese managerial system in the ASEAN region; and
4) Validation of the data we have used and the conclusions we have derived from our case studies of specific Chinese companies and businessmen in the ASEAN region.

Assuming the acceptance of our proposition that the business policy framework best explains the economic behavior and performance of the Overseas Chinese, areas for possible research would be:
1) Speculating on the future business strategies and management practices of the Overseas Chinese in the ASEAN region;
2) Evaluating the implication of such framework on the effectiveness of present and future public policies;
3) Drawing some lessons and principles for application to the broader study of management in developing countries; and
4) Placing such research approach and findings in the present body of business research knowledge specifically in the area of International Business.

The future business strategies and management practices of the Overseas Chinese in the ASEAN region should be of interest to several groups. One such group consists of management scholars who foresee the eventual rise of managerial capitalism world-wide, especially in the free market economies of Southeast Asia. It would be interesting to see if the entrepreneurial spirit of the Overseas Chinese firm which has been firmly lodged in the Chinese family will pass on to the Chinese firm and Chinese professional managers. On a more practical bases, the future business strategies and management practices of the Overseas Chinese should be of great interest to other business organizations in the region. Their future strategies would have to be shaped by the expected strategy of this very significant economic presence in the region. Lastly, the future business strategies of the Overseas Chinese would have to be studied by public policy makers whose public policies in the past have greatly shaped the business strategies of the Overseas Chinese in the region.

This study should be of interest to public policy makers in the region simply because it provides feedback on the effectiveness and unintended effects of their policies. There are several areas worth pursuing.

Past public policies have indicated a poor grasp of the business operations of Chinese firms. For example, public policy makers have always assumed that the Chinese traders (middleman is the pejorative designation) were successful because of their profit margin (usually called "indecent profits") and their high interest rates (usually called "usurious rates"). Thus they have sought to form cooperatives whose expected function is to benefit from those substantial profit margins and to split with the borrowers the savings in interest expense. Of course the nature of the operation of the cooperative places them at a strategic advantage vis-a-vis the Chinese trader. Where the Chinese traders generates volume by handling several products and many suppliers, the cooperative restricts volume by focusing only on its members and their limited products. Where the Chinese trader follows the strategy of economies of scope in an economic environment lacking in infrastructure (i.e. transportation, warehousing, credit system based on barter, etc.), the cooperatives follow a business strategy of specialization which presumes an economic environment strong in infrastructure facilities.

Another example is the understandable unconsciousness of the effect of structure, especially government structure on strategy. The structure of government affects the effectiveness of policy in several ways. Since the government is a multi-objective and multi-divisional organization, there have been numerous instances of the single-objective and unified command organization of the Chinese firm enjoying a competitive advantage. While one bureau is vigorously implementing policies detrimental to the Chinese businessman (i. e. nationalization of retail trade), another bureau in the same department may be vigourously assisting the Chinese businessman (i.e. an investor in a pioneering industry) with low-cost credit and tax subsidies. On the other hand, seeking to coordinate the objectives and policies of the various government units can only result in red tape which puts the local businessmen at a competitive disadvantage vis-a-vis the Chinese businessmen.

My findings point to an alternative approach to the development of indigenous managerial systems. For example, an intensive effort has been going on in the government, academic, and private sectors of the ASEAN countries to define and articulate a Malay managerial system. Our study of the Chinese managerial system would seem to indicate that a prior research question must be asked: what is the Malay business strategy? So long as no Malay business strategies (or preferably as with the Chinese, multi-level generic strategies) are defined and tested in the marketplace, defining and articulating a Malay managerial system would be difficult to achieve and meaningless even if achieved.

As one possible starting point for defining the Malay business strategies, one could point to the difficult strategic posture in which Malay businessmen find themselves (Figure VII-1). Defining the market in terms of two characteristics, commodity/product and low margin/high margin, one would find the Malay businessman in the most uncompetitive position. In effect, if he dealt in a commodity, his price would be too high while if he dealt in a product, his quality would be too cheap.

I propose two possible uses for this research effort. The first is the testing of managerial hypothesis in terms of their applicability to the separate and distinct managerial system described here. The applicability of this book on business groups in a developing country to

FIGURE VII-1
THE STRATEGIC POSTURE OF THE MALAY BUSINESS

	Commodity	Product
Low Margin	Chinese	Japanese
High Margin	Malay	American

the Chinese managerial system is an example of such test. The other is the possible rise of managerial capitalism among Chinese firms. This knowledge may also provide a basis for correcting the built-in bias (in favor of the Western managerial system) of the comparative management analysis approach. By evaluating managerial systems in relation to the business strategies being pursued, comparative management analysis could have an alternative bias-free method of evaluating managerial effectiveness.

In conclusion, it should be noted that while this book may have documented how culture-bound management is, it has also demonstrated how universal the business policy framework can be.